The Road to Someplace Better

The Road to Someplace Better

From the Segregated South to Harvard Business School and Beyond

Lillian Lincoln Lambert

with

Rosemary Brutico

WILEY

John Wiley & Sons, Inc.

Published by John Wiley & Sons, Inc., Hoboken, New Jersey
Published simultaneously in Canada

For general information about our other products and services, please contact our Customer Care Department within the United States at (800) 762-2974, outside the United States at (317) 572-3993 or fax (317) 572-4002.

Wiley also publishes its books in a variety of electronic formats. Some content that appears in print may not be available in electronic books. For more information about Wiley products, visit our Web site at www.wiley.com.

Library of Congress Cataloging-in-Publication Data:

Lambert, Lillian Lincoln, date.
 The road to someplace better : from the segregated South to Harvard Business School and beyond / Lillian Lincoln Lambert with Rosemary Brutico.
  p. cm.
 Includes index.
 ISBN 978-0-470-40166-8 (cloth: alk. paper)
 1. Lambert, Lillian Lincoln, 1940– 2. African American women executives—Biography. 3. African American businesspeople—Biography. 4. Centennial One, Inc. I. Brutico, Rosemary, 1954– II. Title.
 HD6054.4.U6L56 2010
 338.7647—dc22
 [B]   2009015960

Printed in the United States of America

10 9 8 7 6 5 4 3 2 1

To two extraordinary forces in my life:
My mother, Arnetha Hobson,
and my mentor, H. Naylor Fitzhugh

CONTENTS

Photograph sections start on pages 127 and 205.

Lillian's story resonated with me because we are contemporaries and entrepreneurs who were born during one of the darkest periods of American history—segregation—and who broke the color barrier in our respective fields. I was a poor city girl from Omaha, Nebraska, who grew up in the projects and, as I like to say, "surrounded by concrete." Lillian was a poor country girl who was raised on a hardscrabble farm in rural Virginia. Although similar circumstances and a common heritage tie us together, Lillian's story has a compelling universal appeal: it's a testament to the transcendental power of the human spirit in the face of adversity.

The Road to Someplace Better is the soul-searching, inspirational journey of a poor black girl who left the farm at the age of eighteen and headed up North in search of her fortune, thereby dashing her mother's long-held hope that her daughter would follow in her own footsteps and go to college. That Lillian's mother was a college-educated black woman in the early twentieth century was in itself an extraordinary achievement.

Lillian's courage, drive, and mettle would be tested time and again as she fought off the forces that surrounded her: racism, sexism, the tedium of menial dead-end jobs, and, most of all, her own illusions of what it meant to succeed and achieve the American Dream. As Lillian grows in self-knowledge, she begins to understand that what she needs does not lie outside her—in wanting and getting—but instead lies deep within her being. Doing an about-face, she comes to the realization that her mother was right all along: "There is no substitute for education, and there are no shortcuts."

As she pursued her academic studies—with loans, scholarships, and part-time jobs—Lillian became keenly aware of another phenomenon: no matter where she was and what challenges she faced, there seemed to be a band of angels—earthly angels in plainclothes attire–surrounding her and giving her encouragement, shelter, and guidance to stay the course. One of these angels turned out to be a distinguished black professor at Howard University who was instrumental in changing the direction of Lillian's life. Seeing the depth of her intelligence and ambition, this professor convinced her that she was Harvard material. This learned man would know, because he himself was Harvard educated, earning an MBA from the school in 1933. His name is H. Naylor Fitzhugh.

Following in her revered professor's footsteps, Lillian went to Harvard Business School and achieved a historic milestone in 1969 as the first black woman to graduate with a Harvard MBA. After graduating from Harvard, she continued to garner historic "firsts" as a black female entrepreneur who founded a company in her garage with just a few thousand dollars. Over the next twenty-five years, Centennial One grew into a $20 million operation with more than twelve hundred employees.

In an age when our youth reveres the lifestyles of the rich and famous as worth emulating, Lillian offers an antidote. She makes us realize that a celebrity-crazed culture produces false role models and false expectations of what the youth of America can realistically achieve and, more important, what is worth achieving.

In this regard, Lillian's personal journey delivers a powerful message, showing us that our true role models are real people who are embedded in our communities. They are touchable, squeezable, huggable, down-to-earth folks without famous names. In short, they are our parents, our ministers, our teachers, our firefighters, our next-door neighbors, and our social workers. They are those who have our best interests at heart and who are willing and eager to offer guidance and hard-won wisdom.

Ultimately, Lillian is living proof of what we can achieve if we open up to God's earthly angels and let them guide us on our life journey. Lillian is a remarkable woman with a remarkable story. She has something to teach us if we are willing to listen.

—Cathy Hughes,
Founder and Chairwoman, Radio One, Inc.

ACKNOWLEDGMENTS

The publication of my memoir has been a journey that involved the support and enthusiasm of many people along the way. To paraphrase a common expression, "It takes a village to write a book." The project started innocently when a fellow Harvard Business School graduate, Tamara Nikuradse (class of 1990), planted the idea by asking me to provide a quote for her own book, *My Mother Had a Dream: African American Women Share Their Mothers' Words of Wisdom,* which was published in 1997.

After our conversation, she said, "Lillian, you should write a book." Although I was flattered, I responded that I knew nothing about writing a book. Besides, I was too busy running my company. Tamara ignored my reservations and referred me to her editor, who showed interest in my story, but we couldn't work out a satisfying arrangement. The proposal was shelved, and I thought that was the end of an interesting idea.

However, that was not meant to be the end. Thanks to Catherine Walsh, a staff writer at Harvard Business School at the time, who resurrected the proposal after she interviewed me for an article about my winning the HBS Alumni Achievement Award. She was the second person to say, "Lillian, you should write a book." This time I was more open to the idea because I had sold my company and now had more time on my hands.

The book project was brought to life when Cathy introduced me to my coauthor, Rosemary Brutico. Over the next two years, Rosemary and I were inseparable as we came to trust and appreciate each other. Rosemary, through her persistent but gentle probing, unearthed the details of my life while wielding her pen. In turn, I gained an appreciation of the writing process, which was at times frustrating and at other times exhilarating. In the end, our collaboration bore fruit, which is a testament to the power of two minds working together as one. Thanks go to Rosemary's husband, Joe Gallagher, who stuck by both of us, offering encouragement as well as constructive criticism as he pored over many drafts.

This book would never have seen the light of day if it weren't for Dr. David Thomas, H. Naylor Fitzhugh Professor of Business Administration at HBS, who put us in touch with our indomitable agent, Helen Rees. Helen took us under her wing, and thanks to her, we found a publisher and our editor extraordinaire, Hana Lane of John Wiley & Sons. Hana pushed us hard, showing us what it's like to work with a master. I also thank Hana for putting Rosemary in touch with Lois B. Morris, another Wiley author who was a beneficiary of Hana's editorial guidance. Lois offered Rosemary encouragement and advice that only an accomplished writer can provide.

So many other people gave texture, heart, and rhythm to my memoir through their interviews. Gratitude and appreciation go to my brothers, Willie John, Weldon, and Clyde (whose death in 2008 was untimely, but his memory and soothing voice lives on in a taped interview); my childhood best friend and cousin, Shirley Winslow; and my cousin Rudolph DePass. Special thanks go to the octogenarian Porter Smith, "the Mayor," who is a walking encyclopedia of information, much of which I had never heard before I met with him. His story of my parents' courtship abides in my heart.

I am indebted to my HBS classmates (class of 1969) Roy Willis and Clif Darden, who contributed critical historical information on the creation of HBS's African American Student Union (AASU), an organization they cofounded on the premise that it would serve as an oasis for HBS's black students. Many thanks go to several HBS classmates who shared their own experiences of the times: Ted Lewis, Carolyn McCandless, Nancy Pitz, Robin Foote, and Patricia Lewis.

Special thanks go to other HBS alumni who have been generous with their time and advice: Ann Fudge (class of 1977), Nancy Lane (class of 1975), and Benaree "Bennie" Wiley (class of 1972).

Other people at HBS were helpful in giving me access to historical information. Meg Gardner, the executive director of the Bert King Foundation, deserves special recognition for always being there for me, never failing to give fresh insights into my lingering questions. Much appreciation goes to Lauryn Hale and Damien Hooper-Campbell (class of 2009 and copresidents of AASU) for carrying the torch of the original AASU founders. It was music to my ears to hear Lauryn exclaim that "AASU is a home away from home."

Grateful thanks to Kenneth Powell (class of 1974) for his leadership in furthering the mission of the black Harvard alumni organization (HBS's African American Alumni Association). I know that if my mentor, H. Naylor Fitzhugh, one of the founders of the organization, were alive today, he'd be very proud of Ken's efforts. Thank you, Ken, for keeping the black alumni connected to a noble cause.

Thank you, Selena Cuffe (class of 2003), for your valuable input as a reader and your courage to pursue your entrepreneurial dreams while serving a higher purpose for your family and the world at large. Where would I be without Trish Cooper, whose friendship during my HBS days was my rock and refuge. She made my days brighter and my memory of those days fonder.

Then there's Anna Pinellas, my lifetime friend and "partner in crime," who brought levity and laughter to my Howard days. So did Maudine Cooper, a Howard classmate who was interviewed for the book. I regret that my lifelong friend and traveling companion, Vivian Harrison, passed away suddenly before her interview was scheduled, but her spirit graces the pages of this book.

Many thanks to my sister-in-law, Anne Johnson, who, in her inimitable style and with unbridled enthusiasm, always seems to connect me to the right people at the right time. Artrianna Morris is another extraordinary connector who is always willing to extend her network to me.

Thanks to Oliver Singleton for providing valuable information for the book and, more important, for keeping the doors of opportunity open to small and minority-owned businesses through his leadership as the executive director of the Metropolitan Business League in Richmond, Virginia.

A number of people whom I knew in the mid-1980s were extremely helpful in collecting valuable information and photos related to the 1988 enactment of a bill that served as an amendment to the Small Business Act to help develop services and programs for women who are small-business owners. They are Susan Peterson, who was a great sounding board and told me about the twentieth anniversary celebration of the act and gave me the names of the contact people for the photos of my testifying before Congress; Emily Reynolds and Olive Rosen, who provided the photos; and Sharon Hadary, who referred me to Laura Henderson. Laura was active in the initial development of the bill and shared with me a wealth of information.

Special thanks to Cathy Hughes for writing the foreword. I am indebted to Cathy's sister and my Sarasota friend, Jackie Woods, for making the introduction. Many thanks to Rose Harper and James Cash, who graciously shared their networks with me and connected me to important people.

Other contributors to my memoir who were interviewed for the book include Maxine Tinsley, my first secretary, and Legusta Floyd, my creative vice president of human resources. I also wish to thank Ido Jamar for providing a photo of her father and my mentor, H. Naylor Fitzhugh—the man who was responsible for changing the course of my life. Special thanks to Steve McLemore, who honored me with a plaque and an original poem that is part of the book.

Last but not least, thanks from the bottom of my heart to my daughters, Darnetha and Tasha, who have been just the support and encouragement I needed during this period of introspection.

They never failed to help me recollect and relive their childhood events and experiences.

Finally, loving thanks and gratitude go to my husband, Johnny, who lived through this experience on a daily basis. If I am his queen, as he refers to me, then he is my king.

Prologue

Be the change you want to see in the world.

— Mahatma Gandhi

I'm in a taxi heading for 72nd Street and Madison Avenue on New York City's tony Upper East Side. It's October 1986, a clear but chilly evening and the streets are just as busy as they were when I worked as a maid on Fifth Avenue nearly thirty years earlier. As I considered my circumstances then and now, it struck me how much I had changed and how much the world had changed since the late 1950s.

The purpose of my trip this time was to attend a reception hosted by a member of the Committee of 200, a group established in 1982 by a small cadre of powerful businesswomen to expand the agenda of the National Association of Women Business Owners (NAWBO), which was formed in 1975. One of the committee's goals was to use its members' clout to raise money for the association. The reception that evening was not a fundraiser but rather a social gathering to bring together Committee 200 members who lived in the mid-Atlantic region of the country. I was asked to join this prestigious group because I had received positive publicity as a female entrepreneur in the first eight years that I had been in business. Many awards had come my way, including the Small Business Person of the Year for the State of Maryland, which I received in 1981.

In preparing for this trip, I had wanted to make sure that I looked the part of a successful businesswoman, so I chose my outfit carefully. My tailored navy blue knit suit and my mink coat were perfect for the occasion. This time I was ready for New York City.

The cab pulled up to a tall, elegant apartment building where a doorman stood outside like a sentinel guarding his post. He approached the taxi, opened the door, and guided me into the building. After I told him the name of the resident I was visiting, he directed me to the elevator. I quickly scanned my surroundings and flashed back to the wealthy family on Fifth Avenue. This apartment building looked every bit as grand.

I rang the doorbell of the apartment and was greeted by an elderly woman, who, I later learned, was the mother of the hostess and was visiting her daughter. She took my coat, looked at it strangely, and then looked at me. I followed her across the foyer, expecting to be led to the living room, where the reception was being held. Instead, she brought me to the kitchen. It dawned on me what had just happened. I looked at her in disbelief and said, "I'm a guest." Her face turned pale, as if all the blood had just drained from her body. She had assumed, because I am black, that I was there to serve the party. She obviously had missed her cue: my outfit was not one that a maid or a caterer would wear to an affair like this.

In that instant, I was hurled back in time to the 1950s, living in the South, when black people were "put in their place." Part of me was fuming, but at the same time I understood why this woman had done what she did. Her drawl gave her away: she was an elderly white southerner who in her whole life had probably never seen a black person in any other role than a subservient one. This did not make it right, but that's what race has come to mean in America. It's a perfect example of the danger of making assumptions about people based solely on their appearance and, in my case, on the color of my skin.

As soon as her daughter heard about this faux pas, she rushed to my rescue, apologizing profusely for her mother's action. I accepted her apology—what else could I do?—and tried to make the best of an embarrassing moment. For the rest of the evening, I could not seem to get out of the hostess's mother's sight. I knew that she was trying to make me feel welcome, but her gestures, which were an attempt to make amends, were overbearing and, frankly, annoying. There are some actions that you can't take back. This was one of them. It was up to me to look past it, and I did the best I could.

I spent the rest of the evening enjoying myself and getting to know the other women. I didn't pick up any signs from them that they were surprised to see me there. These women were part of a new generation of working women, which made all the difference. This elderly southern lady had made me realize how much progress black women have made as a sex and a race. She also made me realize how much further we had to go before women and minorities would achieve full equality and acceptance. My only consolation that night was that I saw her as a dying breed—or was she?

Putting the evening and the Committee of 200 behind me, I returned to Maryland to concentrate on my business. Although I maintained my membership with the group for a few years, I made a conscious decision to keep a low profile. Perhaps the New York City scene affected me more than I was willing to admit. I decided to look for other opportunities to help improve the socio-economic status of professional women and black people.

The perfect opportunity came my way in April 1988. NAWBO approached its members and other prominent businesswomen and asked us to testify before the Small Business Committee of the U.S. House of Representatives. Gillian Rudd, then president of the association, had contacted Rep. John J. LaFalce (D-NY) to seek his support in sponsoring a bill. The bill was an amendment to the Small Business Act that called for the establishment of programs and initiatives to further the development of small-business concerns owned and controlled by women. Congressman LaFalce introduced the bill (HR 5050) on July 14, 1988, and it became law (Public Law No. 100-533) on October 25, 1988. Our testimonials had paid off.

Based on information that NAWBO provided to me about what it wanted to accomplish during this hearing, I prepared my testimony, detailing my experiences and needs as a business-woman. The day of the testimony was exhilarating. There I was, along with other businesswomen, fighting for women's equal rights and greater opportunities in the world of work. As I waited to present my testimony, I thought back to my days at Harvard Business School and my struggle to prepare myself for a world that was only just beginning to accept professional women in the workforce. Nevertheless, a question haunted me: While still facing the challenges of a woman in business, how long will I also have to endure the challenges as a black woman in business? My struggle is what I call the "double minority complex."

As I gave my testimony, I looked into the faces of the congressional representatives in front of me and saw that they were listening intently. This was not only a personal milestone but also a milestone for my race and my sex. The fight for equality is gained in small victories like this one. I savored the moment; then, feeling freer than ever, I released it.

*   *   *

I could never have imagined that twenty years later I would bear witness to one of the greatest historic moments not only in my lifetime but also in the history of our country. On November 4, 2008, I, along with millions of Americans, celebrated the election of Barack Obama as the first black president of the United States. In that instant, the dream of Martin Luther King Jr. was revealed in a man whose first name, Barack, means "blessed." Spoken forty-five years earlier, Reverend King's words are a stunning reminder of how far we've come as a nation and a people: "I have a dream that one day this nation will rise up and live out the true meaning of its creed: 'We hold these truths to be self-evident, that all men are created equal.'"

As several hundred thousand Americans gathered in Grant Park in Chicago to celebrate this historic milestone, what I saw on TV that night was a melting pot of humanity in which people of all ages and colors from all walks of life linked hearts, minds, and souls for a single purpose: to rejoice in a new president and a renewed patriotism about what it means to be an American.

President Obama said it best in his victory speech: "If there is anyone out there who still doubts that America is a place where all things are possible; who still wonders if the dream of our founders is alive in our time; who still questions the power of our democracy, tonight is your answer. . . . It's the answer spoken by . . . Americans who sent a message to the world that we have never been a collection of red states and blue states; we are, and always will be, the United States of America."

However, even though the election of the first black president reflects a seismic shift in the American consciousness to embrace a more inclusive and tolerant society, black Americans still have a way to go to claim our share of the American Dream. Statistics and recent documentaries tell a grim story of how blacks have lost ground relative to other minorities in our efforts to improve our socioeconomic status.

The disproportionate number of educated black women to educated black men is startling. According to a 2007 *NBC Nightly News* special documentary titled "African-American Women: Where They Stand," nearly two-thirds of black undergraduates are women. At black colleges, the ratio of women to men is 7 to 1. Educational disparity between the sexes is one of the reasons that fewer black women see their male counterparts as potential mates, which could threaten the black nuclear family. The documentary points out that in the past fifty years, the percentage of black women between the ages of twenty-five and fifty-four who have never married has doubled from 20 percent to 40 percent, compared to just 16 percent of white women in this age group who have never married.

Compounding the assault on the black family is the devastation of black men who are falling prey to the ills of society: incarceration, joblessness, drugs, and AIDS. The 2007 *Annual State of Black America* report, published by the National Urban League, concluded: "Empowering black men to reach their full potential is the most serious economic and civil rights challenge we face today. . . . Ensuring their future is critical, not just for the African American community, but for the prosperity, health, and well-being of the entire American family." Essentially, the plight of black men is having a deadly effect on black male teenagers, who without positive male role models are resorting to lives of crime.

Having a black president break through the color barrier couldn't have come at a more critical time for young black Americans, who now have positive proof that they are not limited in their choices of who and what they can be. However, President Obama makes it clear that his presidency is not about race. He emphasized that it's about all of us transcending our self-imposed limitations and embracing a cause for the common good of all Americans. In announcing the creation of the Organizing for America project, President Obama calls on each of us, individually and collectively, to take up the charge to make America a stronger and more just society.

I have chosen to do my part by working with elementary schoolchildren. One particular event that tugged at my heart-strings was a book drive in Sarasota, Florida, where I worked to provide books to underprivileged children, many of whom don't have books to read for pleasure. I remember how much I enjoyed reading as a young girl even though I didn't own any books, and I want to help other children in similar circumstances experience the joy of owning and reading books.

In addition, I have begun to speak around the country, using my own personal story as an example of what can be accomplished when one is willing to unleash the human spirit and envision a better world outside oneself. Although the journey is not easy, as my story shows, the rewards of overcoming obstacles and striving to reach one's full potential will outweigh the trials, tribulations, and challenges.

There is a saying that "Life is 10 percent what happens to you and 90 percent how you respond to it." With the courage of one's convictions and the fortitude to persevere in the face of adversity, I honestly believe that the human spirit can transform the world. We see it happening every day.

1

The Farm

Parents need to fill a child's bucket of self-esteem so high that the rest of the world can't poke enough holes in it to drain it dry.

—Alvin Price

Mother and I had an inside joke. I'd say, "Mama, I know you didn't plan to have me, but that's okay because I know you love me anyway." Mother would simply laugh and reply, "Stop talking crazy." Although I never knew the full story, I was satisfied because Mama's love was straight from the heart. In fact, I was born on Mother's Day, and I believe that she saw me as a special gift from God. That belief has influenced my sense of self from a young age. I came to think that God had a master plan for me, particularly when I recently reflected on an incident that occurred when I was about five years old, as told to me by my brother Willie John.

One of the ways my father earned a living was by selling pulpwood to sawmills. Cutting down trees was considered men's work, so my brothers typically accompanied him into the woods. On this particular day, however, my mother decided to give them a hand, so my older sister, Hattie, and I went with her. Mother gave Hattie, who was sixteen years old, clear instructions to watch me while everyone worked. Being the inquisitive, restless type, I wandered away from the site and found a stump to sit on. Suddenly, there was a loud rumbling sound as a tree fell to the ground only six inches from where I was sitting. My mother screamed in horror, certain that I would be struck dead. According to Willie John, there was no way that I could have survived the weight of the tree had it landed on me. This makes me think that God spared my life in accordance with his plan.

As a child I loved to hear my mother tell me how she carried me in her arms, walking long distances to attend church services or to visit a friend who had given birth to a little girl about a month after Mama gave birth to me. I'd get a thrill from the story of Mrs. Sarah Epps, an elderly black lady, who often remarked in a rather unflattering tone, "Here comes Netta with all those little chicks behind her." Not even Mrs. Epps's remarks could deter Mother from taking her five children places. I admired her for her determination to expose us to things beyond the farm, which for a black woman in the 1940s was an act of courage. No white person—or black person, for that matter—was going to cramp my mother's freedom. Mama had her own way of getting around the limitations of time and place, bending the code of Jim Crow to suit her fancy. Little did she know that her bold steps would instill in her daughter an insatiable love of travel and adventure. That's how all my restless rumblings and grand ideas got started. I followed in Mama's footsteps, and I had big shoes to fill.

*   *   *

Ballsville, Virginia, was a sleepy farming village that would make a perfect drawing for a children's storybook. The simple illustration would show a paved single-lane road that cuts right through the center of town, two country stores, a post office, and a handful of people engaged in their daily activities: talking, shopping, and walking about town. The population of Ballsville was so small that you could almost count the number of people by hand. In fact, when I recently spoke with the local historian, eighty-nine-year-old Porter Smith, who is affectionately called "the Mayor," to gather some facts for the writing of this book, I asked him if he knew what the population of Ballsville was in 1940.

Without hesitation, he responded: "It was two hundred people. The reason I know is that I was in the army stationed in India, and when I told them I was from Ballsville, one of the guys went to get some kind of report, and when he came back, he said, 'Nobody lives there, only two hundred people.'"

After my meeting with the Mayor, my brother Willie John and I did our own count of families who lived in Ballsville back then. We counted exactly 245 people: 165 blacks, representing thirty-five families, and 80 whites, representing twenty-six families. Not only did we come up with an exact count, but we had fun recalling all the family names and picturing exactly where they lived.

Back then, that single-lane paved road through the town was Ballsville's Route 13, which today is called Old Buckingham Road. The two country stores, Netherland's and Dandridge's, were housed in somewhat shabby wooden-frame structures. Dandridge's still exists today, but it goes by a different name, "Do Drop In." There's something about rural hospitality that never changes.

On the surface, everything worked like clockwork in this farming village. The townspeople took efficient, measured steps, shopping at their favorite country store, going to the post office, and waiting for the Greyhound bus to take them to the big city of Richmond, about fifty miles east. Below the surface, however, was an underpinning that worked like a magnetic grid snapping everyone firmly in place. Blacks and whites coexisted and were cordial to one another when their paths crossed, but black people could go only so far until segregation snapped us back in place. Whites were always addressed formally as "Mr." and "Mrs."; blacks were simply called by their first names. Since it was futile to even think about how life should or could be any different, black people lived on the surface just to keep things running smoothly in this small, sleepy farming community.

Although the country stores were owned by white people, the shopkeepers gladly opened their doors to black people because when it came to commerce, money was money. Both white men and black men owned farms, but the land of a white farmer was invariably bigger, yielding more (but not necessarily better) crops than a black man's farm did. Unfortunately, black families who didn't own farms worked as hired hands on white people's farms: the men as farmhands, the women as domestics.

The dark forces of racism swirled around blacks during election time as well. Most southern states levied a poll tax, which was enacted as a way of barring poor blacks from registering to vote. My parents were able to pay the poll tax, and they always made sure that they exercised their hard-earned right to vote. Although Pa couldn't write, he would sign his name with an X. The poll tax was finally abolished with the enactment of the Twenty-fourth Amendment in 1964.

*   *   *

I can only imagine my parents' shock when, in late 1939, they learned that a new baby was expected six months before my mother's forty-first birthday. For a forty-eight-year-old subsistence farmer who already had four children by Mama—Hattie (eleven), Willie John (ten), Weldon (almost seven), and Clyde (eighteen months)—my arrival was probably not a cause for celebration. This was in addition to Pa's two children, Henry and Elvira, by his first wife, who died when their children were young. By the time I was born, Henry and Elvira were young adults and had moved to Riverhead, New York, to live with my father's relatives. It was only in later years that I became close to Henry, whom I saw more as an uncle than a brother. I never got to know Elvira, who was institutionalized before I was born.

I, Lillian Novella Hobson, the fifth and last child of Willie D. and Arnetha B. Hobson, was born on May 12, 1940, at home in Ballsville. A midwife delivered me, which was the customary practice because the closest hospital was in Richmond, about fifty miles away. However, it was more than distance that necessitated a home birth: a hospital stay was too expensive.

My birthplace was a simple farmhouse that was set back from a dirt road on thirty acres of land about a mile from the main road. The house was built by my maternal grandfather, Grandpa

John, after my parents had gotten married. Many years later, when I began to question why things were the way they were, I asked Mama, "Why did you allow Papa to bring you so far back in the woods?" Her response was, "Land's cheaper off the main road."

When I asked the question, I was specifically referring to the dirt road that was notorious for the problems it caused in foul weather, particularly when it rained. Car wheels would spin and get stuck in the dirt, and people's shoes would get caked with mud when they traveled the road. Even my mother's good friend, who was always willing to drive Mama wherever she needed to go (my mother never learned to drive), refused to drive down the road after it had rained for fear of getting stuck in the thick red clay.

Without my mother knowing it, the response she had given me answered another question I had been pondering. I had a curious mind, and I was always looking for cues to explain the social order of our world. Whenever I understood the answer, I'd say to myself, *Aha! That explains it.* Mama's answer to my question that day, tossed off in a cavalier manner, explained to me how my father came to own land, and I understood something more about the workings of Jim Crow. I learned that desirable and better-appointed land (right off the main road) was owned by white folks, so I concluded that Pa was able to buy land that no one else wanted—as Mama had said, cheap land.

The day I figured it out, I became even more proud of my dad. He worked the land hard and made the land work for him, growing tobacco as the family's main source of income. I also got a new insight into Pa: not only was he a good father and a good husband, but he was also a good provider.

When I met with Porter Smith, the Mayor, I asked him if he knew how my parents had met. If anyone would know, he would. After all, he was there. In a spirited, mumbling old voice that was barely audible, he regaled me with the story of my parents' courtship, but not without first telling me that my mother was the meanest schoolteacher he ever had.

"She made us write sentences on tests when we were used to true and false and multiple choice," he said. "She even flunked a student." I smiled, although I questioned his word choice ("meanest"), but I knew what he meant. My mother was a disciplinarian, and she set high standards. She didn't cut you any slack if she thought you were lazy, thoughtless, or unprepared.

According to the Mayor, it was customary for the townsmen to offer transportation to the teachers to and from school. My father used this custom to his advantage and offered to be of assistance to my young mother in her efforts to get to school. Since her parents lived in the next town, Mohemenco—about twenty miles away—my mother couldn't stay with them because the walk to Ballsville Elementary would have been too long a trek. Nevertheless, as you might expect of this industrious farming community, there was a practical solution to every problem. New teachers were encouraged to board at the homes of the local teachers. Mama ended up boarding with Mrs. Sadie Hopkins, who taught first through third grades.

Imagine the excitement my father, a recent widower, must have felt when he heard the news that a young single teacher had recently moved to Ballsville. Teaching was held in high esteem, and snagging a teacher as your spouse was considered a very good catch. In addition, my mother was a rarity; there weren't many black women in the early twentieth century who had college degrees. My mother had graduated from Virginia Normal and Industrial Institute in 1922, which today is known as Virginia State University.

Knowing my father, I'm sure he approached my mother with great confidence. He must have; how else would a man with a third-grade education be able to impress a college-educated schoolteacher? I suspect that he waited for a rainy day to make his move, riding up to the school grounds in his horse and buggy at the start of the school year—just to be sure no one beat him to it—tipping his hat and greeting my mother.

After learning the name of this young lady, he probably said, "Good afternoon, Miss Hobson. It is raining too hard for a lady to walk in the rain. Let me take you home." How could she refuse? I can see him now: neatly dressed, clean shaven, and courteous—drawing on all the mannerisms of a fine gentleman. Underneath it all, I suspect my pa had an ulterior motive that day. With two teenage children still living at home with him, he knew that they could all use a woman's touch around the house.

Knowing Mama as I do, I'm sure she had her own motive for accepting a ride from a stranger, albeit a widower. I suspect she was afraid of being an old maid if she did not find a suitable prospect soon. After all, she was in her late twenties, which at that time was considered old to be unmarried.

The rest, as they say, is history. My parents married in 1928 and set up house. My mother did not even have to change her surname. The odd fact is that my parents had the same last name, Hobson, but they were not related. When my siblings and I asked about it, my parents would simply reply that there were three sets of black Hobsons in Powhatan County, none of whom was related. To complicate matters, when we children applied for our Social Security cards, our applications were always returned with our mother's maiden name highlighted and with instructions to correct the error. We stopped questioning the origin of the Hobson name after a while; that's just the way it was.

By the time I came along, Mama no longer taught school. The demands of taking care of her children outweighed the demands of teaching, so she had to make a decision. Family came first. However, she still had to help my father make ends meet, so she cleaned and cooked for white folks in their homes three days a week. "Day's work," as it was called, gave her the flexibility to work as many or as few days as she wanted so she could also take care of her family.

*   *   *

Farm life in the rural South was made even harder by the shackles of segregation rattling around us—sometimes reaching a deafening pitch that could startle us awake from a good night's sleep. Nevertheless, my parents knew instinctively how to make their children feel safe, to dispel our fears, and to let us be carefree. They gathered beams of hope from the sky, the constellations, the sun, the moon, the trees, and the earth and poured them into our hearts and our souls. My parents loved us up to God, and God in turn showed us how to use our feet as wings, our hands as tools, and our minds as transformers.

So what if our farmhouse was an odd shape that bent to the contours of the uneven terrain? Grandpa John Hobson, my mother's father and a part-time carpenter, had to build the house on three-foot stilts in some sections and level to the ground in other sections because he didn't have the heavy equipment necessary to make the land level. Although this two-story, eight-room, box-shaped, white-painted, wooden frame didn't look like much, my younger brother Clyde and I endowed it with magical qualities.

Underneath the raised section of our odd-looking farmhouse, we played and laughed for hours. Like most young boys, Clyde had a fascination with cars, and as his younger and dutiful sister, I was recruited to help him create his dream cars. I was glad to oblige because I knew that I would reap the reward of driving my very own fantasy car. The materials we used to construct our cars were flat wooden boards (about six inches wide and twelve inches long) and some of Mama's empty thread spools (about two inches high).

Clyde's creative mind went to work as he issued instructions to me: "Lay the board flat, then center the nail at the top of the board and nail it in with the hammer. Now slide the empty spool over the nail, and you have your steering wheel." Since the space beneath the farmhouse was too low for us to stand up in, we'd get down on our hands and knees and push the cars along the ground. The best part of all was pretending that we were driving on highways made of asphalt, not the dirt roads we were used to living near. We'd pretend that we were running errands in town, visiting friends, or heading for the "big city." What a thrill it was.

Although I formed easy-going bonds with my three brothers—they seemed to enjoy looking after their little sister—this was not the case with my older sister, Hattie, who moved to Richmond to work as a domestic when she was seventeen. Although I longed to have an older sister to look up to, Hattie did not see herself in that role. She preferred to keep her distance from the family. In fact, I often overheard my parents say that they had no idea where she was from time to time. It was only a few years before she died at the age of sixty-six that we finally bonded as sisters.

Just as Clyde's and my fantasy world set us free, the rituals and rigors of everyday life grounded us in reality. I like to think that our self-care routine was the way we built character. We had high hopes that one day our father would convert one of the small rooms upstairs into a bathroom, according to Grandpa's instructions, but Pa never got around to installing indoor plumbing. All families develop their own folklore to explain away odd behavior or strange expressions. In our case, we always referred to the designated room as the bathroom even though it was nothing more than a storage room.

It's hard to know whether Pa didn't have the money to build a bathroom or he just didn't see the need for such a luxury, but we did what we had to do. We used an outhouse during the day and a potty—what we called a "slop jar"—at night, which we disposed of in the morning. Saturday was declared "bath day." After all, there was no way that you'd want to have a dirty body when you went to church on Sunday, which in the black community was considered the most important day of the week.

The bath ritual began by heating water on a wood-burning stove and then pouring it into a large, round, gray tin tub. We were all expected to prepare our own bathwater, with the understanding that each person was responsible for dumping out the used water and cleaning the tub for the next person. We bathed with military precision—a quick step in, a quick step out—because no one wanted to linger in a tub that was too small to move around in. As I grew older, the once-a-week bath routine felt inadequate, so every night before going to bed, I'd heat a small basin of water and take a sponge bath. Even after I left the farm at the age of eighteen, my folks continued to use the tin tub and the outhouse.

I'll never forget the day we got electricity. I was eight years old, and I ran through the house flicking every switch just to see if the lights would really come on. Hallelujah! It was like coming out of a dark cave and being hit by the blinding sun. To think that I could now read and do my homework without hunching over a kerosene lamp, or that I could go from one room to another without having to carry a lamp.

It would be another four years before we traded in our icebox for a refrigerator. What a glorious appliance; we no longer had to rely on the iceman's weekly delivery or worry that our meat and vegetables would go bad. There was one modern appliance that Mama just couldn't adjust to, however—the electric stove. She swore that food never tasted as good as it did when it was cooked on a wood-burning stove. We never did get rid of our potbellied stoves, which remained our source of heat—one in the kitchen and one in the dining room.

Only my parents' bedroom and a guest bedroom had stoves to generate heat. For the rest of us, going to bed on cold winter nights was like walking into a refrigerator. I remember well how quickly I would undress, as if performing a quick-change act at the circus. I wouldn't even bother to hang up my clothes. Instead, I'd throw them on top of the bed to add additional warmth to the pile of quilts Mama had made to keep her children warm. Central heating was never ours to have.

*　　*　　*

My parents were as different as night and day, and their opposite personalities and contrary opinions would have been their undoing had their commitment to their marriage and raising a family not been as strong as it was. They had a singular focus, which was to work and provide for their children as husband and wife, no matter what. I'm reminded of the marriage covenant as expressed in the Bible: "What God has joined together, let no man put asunder." My siblings and I were the beneficiaries of this unbreakable bond, which, in my view, was a gift. In fact, I have come to see my parents' indestructible union as a source of strength that gave me the confidence and courage to leave the farm and make a life for myself.

Papa was not a large man—he was about five feet eight inches, somewhat muscular and stocky, with broad features—but he cast a large shadow. I'd say he was hardnosed and strong willed, and he could be unapproachable if he was in a bad mood. The Mr. Tough Guy, I'm-in-charge image was strong in him, and we all knew where we stood. There was work that women did and work that men did, or so Papa thought.

For example, he didn't think my brothers should do housework. Despite his objections, my brothers learned how to cook, clean, wash, and iron. The truth was we all hated farmwork, and we'd do anything—even housework—not to have to work in the fields pulling suckers (shoots from the lower part of a plant's stem) and fat green worms off the tobacco leaves. However, we all understood the drill: if Pa had to get up at the crack of dawn and be in the tobacco field by five o'clock, the rest of us had to rise and shine with him. To hear Pa say "Get up even if you just sit by the fire" always drove me crazy. What a ridiculous demand, but I would never dare to challenge him on that front.

Like a crack that lets in light, there was a crack in Pa's chiseled facade that allowed me to creep into his soft spot and stroke his big heart. For example, whenever I'd ask him if he would drive me to the house of my cousin, Shirley Taylor, on his way to the country store, he would respond in a gruff tone, "No, I don't know if I am going." I knew that he was going, however, because he went almost every night. So I'd walk away quietly and not make a fuss. Then, as soon as he was ready to leave, he'd come over to me and say, "Sis, are you ready to go?" Of course I was ready because I already knew that he'd go and would take me to Shirley's if I just gave him time to think about it.

I think that Pa took a special liking to me because we both liked money and the way it made us feel. My brother Willie John loves to tell how Pa would bribe me to help him work in the tobacco field at harvest time. The harvest was the one time during the year that men, women, and children were expected to lend a hand in the fields. No questions were asked, no exceptions were made.

As Willie John says, "Pa told Lillian that if she helped in the tobacco field, he would give her some money when he sold the crop. So after he sold his tobacco, he gave her twenty-five dollars and told her if she helped next year, he'd give her more. True to his word, the next year he gave her twenty-six dollars. We all laughed and teased her and said, 'Boy, that's some kinda raise, Lillian.'" I may have been the butt of my family's joke, but Papa instilled in me the value of making a living and the feeling of independence that comes from having money in your pocket.

Then there was Mama. She was as soft spoken as my father was gruff. I loved hearing her sweet singing voice float through the air as she worked around the house. She was of medium build, five feet three inches, with a smooth brown complexion. I always envied her full head of beautiful, thick, straight, black hair, which she wore in a pageboy. Although she was a woman of few words, when she did speak, her words could cut right through you if you couldn't bear to hear the truth.

For instance, when Mom was in the hospital at the age of eighty-five, one of the nurses said to her, "Mrs. Hobson, you look so good for your age. What did you do to keep yourself looking so good?" Mom responded, "I always took care of myself." To this the nurse responded, "I'd better start taking care of myself." Without batting an eye, my mother replied, "I think it's too late." When the nurse left the room, Mom curled up in a ball and laughed her heart out. I was somewhat taken aback and exclaimed, "Mom, I can't believe you said that to the nurse!" When she was able to get control of her laughter, she simply replied, "Well, it's true."

Mother performed a critical role in our family: she was the chief disciplinarian. When the children were naughty, it was Mama who wielded the switch, which was a twig from a tree. Major infractions were lying, disobeying, being disrespectful (especially to our elders), and fighting with siblings. Today I jokingly remark that if the laws about child abuse had been in effect when we were children, most of my generation's parents, including Mama, would be in jail. That might be an exaggeration, because we were not physically abused, but she didn't hesitate to spank us when she thought we deserved it.

Although Mama didn't really hurt us, we'd pretend that she did: we'd holler and jump around the room as if she were beating us mercilessly. It was a joke, though, because her whippings were like feather taps compared to Pa's form of punishment. You never wanted to be fussed at by Pa because it never seemed to end. After scolding you, he'd scowl at you for what seemed like an eternity. That would hurt more than any whipping ever could.

Mom's use of the switch was curious. She'd order us (mainly Clyde and me because the others at that point had already left home or were too old to spank) to go into the woods and bring back a switch. In later years, Clyde and I laughed at how we were ordered to play an instrumental role in choosing our own tool for being disciplined. It's like asking someone to select a weapon by which to be executed. Clyde often commented, "If that wasn't the dumbest thing. Can you imagine askin' a child to find a switch for his own whippin'?"

At the time, I didn't see the humor or absurdity of the switch, but Clyde did. Clyde was clever that way. He would emerge from the woods and hand Mama the smallest branch he could find.

Mother would shake her head, look disapprovingly at it, and order him to go back and get a "decent-size" one. So Clyde would march back into the woods, shaking his head back and forth, and chuckling to himself as if to say, "I thought I'd get away with that." He'd then re-emerge, carrying a switch that was only slightly larger than the previous one.

The switch ritual brought out my mother's and Clyde's unique sense of humor, which to this day brings a smile to my face when I think of a particular incident. One day when Mama was whipping Clyde, he decided to return the favor. While she belted him with the switch, he turned and began smacking her behind with his right hand. Mama couldn't refrain from laughing, so she cut the whipping short, left the room, and let out a good, hearty laugh until she started to cry. I used to love to watch Mama laugh. She'd laugh until big tears rolled down her beautiful round face.

My parents could smooth over most of their differences, except when it came to school and farmwork, which made sense given their educational backgrounds. As soon as the harvest season came around, the "harvest dance" would begin.

It would go something like this: Pa would announce to Clyde and me in the early morning, usually just as we were getting dressed for school, "You can't go to school today. I need you to help me in the 'bacco." We'd immediately run over to Mother and say, "Pa wants us to stay home and work in the tobacco. We can't stay home." That would be her cue to come to our rescue. She'd approach our father and say, "Willie, you really shouldn't keep the children out of school to work on the farm. They need to get their education."

Clyde and I would be in earshot of their conversation. Keeping our fingers crossed that Mom would win, we'd turn to each other with puzzled looks on our faces and say, "Why does he keep doing this?" Mother won some of the battles and she lost others, but Clyde and I won the ultimate battle. It was when we were in high school that we finally figured out a strategy.

After missing a few days of school in the early fall, we decided to do something about it. Our teacher, Mrs. Freddie Finney, planted the seed. She was very strict about giving tests. If you missed a test in her class, she wouldn't let you make it up the way some of the other teachers would. We kept her in mind the day we approached Pa. On that particular harvest morning, Clyde and I steeled ourselves. If you had looked at us from the inside, you would have seen two terrified kids, but we weren't about to show our feelings, least of all to Pa.

Clyde spoke first. "Pa, we can't stay home today. We're missin' too much time from school. Plus, Lillian and I both have tests today." I was in the background, punctuating his words with "Yes! Yes!" With a shocked look on his face, Pa relented and uncharacteristically said, "Okay, you can go to school today." We were stunned that he backed down so quickly, but maybe he was surprised that we had the nerve to defy him. We had finally figured out how to summon a higher power that Pa respected.

From that day on, whenever Papa asked us to stay home from school to work in the fields, we were always able to convince him otherwise. Finally, Pa just stopped asking. I like to think that he was finally beginning to understand the value of an education.

*   *   *

Class is a strange phenomenon in this country. We know that it exists, but we downplay its importance by spouting platitudes like "Upward mobility is achievable if you're able to pick yourself up by your own bootstraps." There's one thing missing from this equation—at least there was when I was growing up. Back then, upward mobility applied only to white society. I don't profess to speak for the white race, but many white people didn't think of black people as belonging to any class. They just saw us as black and classless. Such ignorance was almost as dangerous as slavery and segregation because it suggested that blacks didn't have the means or the mentality to rise above their environment.

That was a mistaken notion, however. There were different classes of black people. Since farmers didn't make much money or have much in the way of material comforts, my family was considered poor, but there were some families that were even poorer. By contrast, my cousin Shirley's family was considered better off than we were because her parents worked for rich white folks in Riverhead, New York. They had a steady income, unlike my family, who depended on the uncertain income from farming.

Obviously, the better-paying jobs were up North. In this respect, getting ahead for southern blacks came with a price. Shirley's parents left Shirley and her sister, Audrey, in Ballsville with their grandparents, Jenny and Fred Hobson. After Shirley's grandfather died, Grandma Jenny, a strong woman, raised Shirley and Audrey by herself with the love and care of a mother.

Shirley's grandma's home became the main gathering place for many in the black community, particularly after the family got an RCA television set. Shirley's father had been lucky and had won the TV in a raffle when he was visiting Ballsville. Since he already had a TV in New York, he gave this one to his children and his mother-in-law. As a result, Shirley's grandmother opened up her home to the whole neighborhood.

My world was never the same after I saw my first television show. I remember that we'd all gather at Shirley's house on Sunday nights and watch *The Ed Sullivan Show*. My father would reserve a front-row seat on Wednesday nights to watch the fights. His favorite fighter was Joe Louis, who was affectionately known as "the Brown Bomber." Pa would sit there in front of the TV and curl his fists and throw punches in the air, grunting and groaning as if he himself were boxing.

The thing I loved most about Shirley was that she never made me feel inferior when she came back from spending the summer with her folks in New York wearing the latest fashions. She never flaunted the things that her parents were able to provide for her.

I tried not to compare what I had to what other families had, and it worked out well when I was surrounded by my family and my cousins. In fact, I considered myself a happy-go-lucky child until I reached puberty. I don't know what happened to the contented little girl, but suddenly I felt certain that all of the forces of the world had started to gang up on me, and nothing looked right or felt right. I was forever comparing myself to other people, and I never measured up. Some of my uneasy feelings were undoubtedly the result of adolescent growing pains (puberty and happiness don't mix), but I became obsessed to the point that I always felt a thick black cloud looming over me.

Although I was a good student and enjoyed learning very much, I had a hard time adjusting socially. I was ashamed of my hand-me-down dresses and, even worse, the dresses my mother made from fifty-pound burlap feed bags. Wearing clothes like these in front of Shirley was okay, but wearing them in front of other children was humiliating.

I was also bothered by the school lunches Mama prepared. My homemade rolls filled with fruit preserves paled in comparison to my schoolmates' bologna or chicken sandwiches made with store-bought bread. Eating Wonder Bread meant that you could afford to buy bread instead of having to make it from scratch. This made lunchtime particularly painful. I'd put my mouth as close to my lunchbox as I possibly could in the hope that no one could see what I was eating.

As if that wasn't bad enough, I also had to endure recess. We used to play a game that really upset me. We'd all line up and run around the school building as if we were driving cars. As we passed a certain part of the building, we had to call out the type of car we were driving, and it had to be the year and make of the car your family owned. My father drove a ten-year-old clunker, so I'd have to shout out that I was driving an old black Plymouth. Most of the other children's families' cars were no older than three years. I was too self-absorbed to realize that some of the other kids, whose families didn't even own a car, were worse off.

Those kids were excluded from the game, which was the worst kind of humiliation. Even though I wasn't proud of our car, I at least could choose to play the game, and I did because I wanted to be included.

I was also beginning to see my brothers differently around this time. I looked up to them and admired how handsome they were and how popular they were with the girls. Compared to them, I thought I was the ugly duckling in the family. My hair was short, coarse, and hard to manage, whereas my brothers had soft and wavy hair that was easy to comb. They also had the most beautifully shaped eyebrows. As every black woman knows (even to this day), a young girl's hair shapes her self-image far more than it should. I just didn't have "good" hair. Good hair was defined as straight; "bad" hair was defined as kinky. It was most unfortunate.

The only thing that saved me was that I loved to read. It was my escape into another world, far away from Ballsville. Even though our town didn't have a library, I managed to get my hands on reading material, such as *Reader's Digest, Guideposts,* Sunday school books, newspapers, and other magazines. When I became older and my social life was as exciting as that of a church mouse, I couldn't wait for my cousin Evelyn Harris to give me her old, once-read magazines like *True Confessions* and *True Romance.* Pa would become furious when he saw me reading what he considered to be trashy romance magazines. He would turn to my mother and say, "Netta, why are you lettin' her read such trash?" Mama's retort was simple but effective: "Willie, I don't care what Lillian reads as long as she reads."

My love for Daddy was a constant, but my love for Mama was boundless. She was there for me when I least expected it and, at times, when I least deserved it. Our affection for each other probably grew out of necessity because we were surrounded by strong-willed men and we needed to stick up for each other in the spirit of sisterhood. But our bond went much deeper: I sensed in my bones that my mother packed all her dreams in me in the hope that her pioneering spirit would live on in her youngest daughter.

Mama also stuck up for me in ways that only the female sex could appreciate. When I was about twelve years old, Papa gave in and bought Clyde a bicycle. I wasn't exactly jealous, but I did think that Clyde owed it to me to teach me how to ride. However, when I asked him to teach me, which I did over and over, he'd just laugh and taunt me. The bike became a power struggle, and we'd argue over it incessantly.

Finally, my mother got so tired of hearing us carry on that she assigned specific days for each of us to have the bicycle. Even though I didn't know how to ride, that wasn't going to stop me from taking possession of the bike on my assigned days. On those days, I would walk or run with the bike around the yard until I got tired. Just wrapping my hands around the handlebars and pushing the bike around gave me a feeling of accomplishment and power: I'd think, *This is Clyde's bike, and he has to share it with me.* I was also sure that one day I would show them all that I could ride a bike.

I must have become a little cocky because one day I was running down the path pushing the bike alongside me at an incredibly high speed. As I was running toward the front steps of the house, I realized, to my horror, that I couldn't stop the bike. I certainly wasn't about to turn it loose, because I was afraid of damaging it, so I held on to it for dear life. As the bike bounced up the steps, the handlebars hit me in the mouth and broke one of my front teeth. At first I wasn't aware of the extent of the damage, but I ran to Mother with my hand over my mouth and showed her what had happened.

Mama screamed, "What have you done?" She was furious with me because all she could see were dollar signs when she thought about the dental expense she could not afford. This was in sharp contrast to my father's reaction, who didn't see it as a problem at all. He matter-of-factly stated that I could get it fixed when I became an adult. That was a preposterous solution to my mother, and I heard her say to him, "How can I let her—a young girl—grow up with a broken tooth right in the front of her mouth?"

My mother's unfailing love for me pulled through. She worked extra hours to earn the money to get my tooth fixed. That wasn't the end of her Good Samaritan deed, either. The closest dentist was in Farmville, Virginia, which was some forty to fifty miles away. Mom and I had to take the Greyhound bus to get there, which was an additional expense, and since we had to make several trips to get my tooth fixed, the travel costs were even higher.

I've often kidded Clyde that I blame him for that incident because of his refusal to teach me how to ride the bike. By the way, I did learn how to ride a bike shortly thereafter. My brother Weldon took pity on me and taught me the basics. The rest was up to me.

*   *   *

As far as I was concerned, one of Ballsville's major highlights was the Greyhound bus ride to Richmond. The bus passed through our town twice a day like clockwork, leaving for Richmond at about six in the morning and returning to Ballsville around six in the evening. As a preteen, I loved to flag down the bus with Mama to go to Richmond to spend the day shopping (well, more like browsing) in the fancy Richmond department stores, Thalhimer's and Millers & Rhoads.

I remember how difficult it was to fall asleep the night before our shopping trip: I'd lie awake in bed envisioning all the pretty things that we would buy, even though I knew in my heart that our purchases would be practical ones—the kinds of things that Ma and Pa couldn't find in Ballsville, like Sunday clothes for church and household items like linens and dishes.

The day of our Richmond shopping trip, my parents rose earlier than usual so we could have breakfast and get to the main road in time to catch the bus. Papa seldom went with us, but he always made sure that we got off safely. He would drive us to the bus stop and wait with us until the bus arrived. During the winter, Mom and I would often wait for the bus in the warmth of Netherland's, the country store. But we always had to be on the lookout for the bus in order to give ourselves enough time to rush out of the store and wave it down. We had this unsettling feeling that the bus driver would not see us and would zoom right past us if we were even just a minute late. We never once missed the bus.

Our Richmond excursions would have been pure delight, except for one thing. Mama and I would have to walk past rows of empty seats in the front of the bus and sit in the back. When I first became aware of this peculiar behavior, I asked Mother why we could not sit up front. She simply said, "That's the way things are; it's the law." I didn't press her, but I could never understand why the law required us to sit in the back of the bus. I began to harbor feelings of resentment as I passed whites who were sitting up front because I knew that I did not have the same choice. What made it worse was that if a black person sat too close to the front, a white passenger would usually ask the bus driver to tell the black person to move to the back of the bus. As I grew older, I would learn that this kind of arrangement had a name. It was called *segregation*.

I learned much more about segregation, particularly as it applied to the education of black and white children in the South. Ballsville had only one school, Ballsville Elementary, which was designated as the school for black children in grades 1 through 6. No school bus was provided, so we were expected to walk the two miles to and from school. In contrast, the white children in Ballsville were bused to their own elementary school in Powhatan, which was twelve miles away.

After the sixth grade, both black and white children were bused separately to different schools in Powhatan. Black children attended Pocahontas High School, and white children attended Powhatan High School. The bus ride made getting to school more enjoyable, especially when my brothers were substitute drivers. On those days, I felt privileged because I got to ride the bus the whole way—to and from school—because the bus ride started and ended at our house. I learned later, however, that the only reason black kids rode the bus at all was that it would have been unthinkable to expect children to walk the twelve miles to and from Pocahontas High School.

When I was in elementary school, I had to wake up at the crack of dawn to do my chores around the house—making the beds, sweeping the kitchen floor, and washing the dishes—before walking to school. Thank God for my cousin Shirley, who made what could have been a dreadful walk into a pleasant excursion. Sometimes on our way to school, we'd stop by the country store and buy some penny candy—that is, if we could find some spare change. Those were the fun days.

Other days were not much fun, as Shirley recently reminded me. I don't remember how the following incident happened (this is probably my attempt to blot it out of my mind), but it underscores the indignity that black schoolchildren suffered on their walk to school. On occasion, the white kids on the bus would stick their heads out the windows, spit on us, and throw things at us as they passed us. It all came to a head one day when some of the older black boys waited in ambush behind some trees as the rest of us walked ahead. When the white kids began to taunt us, the black boys emerged from the bushes with branches in their hands and started to whack the white kids when they stuck their heads out the windows. The white kids were so shocked that they never bothered us again.

Under segregation, black schools had fewer resources and amenities than white schools did, for no other reason than that they were underfunded by the government. Lack of resources didn't stop us from getting a good education, however. Our teachers' dedication to their students compensated for the meager tools and teaching supplies they had at their disposal. Although our textbooks were often outdated—they were usually used books that the white schools had discarded—our teachers were determined to prepare us for the real world.

I, for one, thrived in an all-black environment because our teachers really cared for the whole person. They were just as concerned about our moral development as they were about our academic achievements. In this regard, our teachers were seen as extensions of our families and our community. They were the same people who attended our churches, who lived in our neighborhood, and, most important, who knew our parents very well, much to the consternation of naughty children.

You never wanted your folks to find out that you had misbehaved at school and that Miss So-and-So had to take disciplinary action. If word got out that a teacher spanked you, it usually resulted in another whipping at home. Although I was too good a student and too shy and obedient to misbehave, I could easily imagine what would have happened if my folks had learned that I had been bad at school.

In my opinion, school integration exacted a price on the quality of education for black students. Although the 1954 landmark decision of *Brown v. Board of Education* was an attempt to redress the effects of racial segregation in education, one of the results of the decision was the loss of many dedicated black teachers and administrators. In many cases, black teachers were replaced by white teachers, who were not part of our community and were not sympathetic to black culture. In short, they were out of their element when it came to understanding and teaching black children.

*   *   *

Life improved dramatically my senior year of high school. This unpopular girl suddenly became popular. I was shocked when I was invited to the prom and even more shocked when Papa let me go. I don't remember much about the prom or my date, but I distinctly remember how elegant I felt in a strapless beige evening gown made of organza and chiffon that my cousin, Estelle Walker, had given me. That was a hand-me-down that I could like. Estelle worked as a maid for the Schwarzschilds—a prominent Richmond family who owned many jewelry stores—and she often gave me fashionable clothes, like the evening gown, that the Schwarzschild daughters didn't want anymore.

Despite my growing popularity, my parents were not keen on my dating. Although I probably could have convinced Mama of the importance of dating as a rite of passage, I wouldn't even think of approaching the subject with Papa. He still had a bad taste in his mouth from an incident that occurred when I was fifteen years old. It involved my cousin Shirley, two sisters who were friends of ours, and me.

One of the sisters was allowed to drive her mother's car to a house party, and we convinced our parents to let us go with them. When we got to the party, however, we became frightened because we saw the sisters' brother, who had been drinking, waving a gun. Shirley and I wanted to leave immediately, but instead of asking the sister who could drive to take us home, we asked two young men at the party if they would.

We didn't see any harm in having these two guys take us home, but apparently my parents and Shirley's grandmother did. It was unacceptable behavior for two young girls to ride in a car at night with two young men, even if we knew them well. When the news got out about what we had done, the adults called a meeting to discuss how to reprimand us. After the meeting, my father turned to me and announced that I would not be allowed to date until I was forty years old.

Although dating was off limits, I found another way of asserting myself and declaring my independence. I would teach myself how to drive. One day I was visiting my aunt, Alberta Harris, and I convinced my cousin Otis to let me drive his car, a 1954 black-and-white Ford. Without batting an eye, he handed me the keys and told me I could drive the car down the dirt road without him. I don't know why he was so willing to give me his car without even asking me if I could drive. I suspect that he thought I wasn't serious about taking the car.

He obviously misjudged me. I took the car and drove it safely down the dirt road and back to the house a number of times. Ever since that day, whenever I visited my aunt, my first request was to drive the car. I did this until I felt confident behind the wheel. Then one day, during my senior year in high school, some of my classmates and I decided to go down to the courthouse to get our driver's licenses.

When I came home that day, I proudly showed my father my license—my act of independence. He looked at it incredulously. When I told him how I had learned to drive, he was stunned. It was as if I had told him that I had taken a trip to the moon. The irony was that even though I had a driver's license, I had nothing to drive. I would be twenty-eight years old before I owned a car. Nonetheless, it was comforting to know that at least I could drive, and in theory I was advancing the freedom of women.

*   *   *

There is one other highlight of my early years in Ballsville, which has to do with the harvest, family, religious instruction, fancy clothes, and a yearning for adventure.

The first Sunday in August was the most important Sunday of the calendar year to this farming community. It was the day of the Big Meeting—also called Revival. At Revival, people were encouraged to renew their spiritual lives. Friends and relatives came from far and near, and many of my uncles, aunts, and cousins came from as far away as New York. Seeing my relatives arrive from the big city was like watching a fashion show. Women came all decked out in fancy, fitted dresses, colorful wide-brim summer hats, and three-inch high heels. The men sported tailored suits, topped off with a hat. Most arrived on the church grounds driving modern, shiny cars with whitewall tires. This scene was enough to suggest to me that there was a better and more prosperous life somewhere beyond the farm.

Revival Sunday was so exciting and so much fun that even fidgety children did not object to the services that were held for most of the day. The first service started at noon and lasted for two or three hours, depending on the length of the sermon; the second service began at four o'clock. In between, dinner was served on the church grounds. Every family set up its own table, offering an array of homemade foods and freshly harvested vegetables to everyone in attendance: fried chicken, roast beef, turkey, collards, turnips, kale, mustard greens, string beans, potato salad, macaroni and cheese, candied sweet potatoes, corn pudding, chocolate cake, pound cake, apple pie, and sweet potato pie. We all made the rounds, sampling food from everyone's table.

A guest minister was always invited to "carry on" Revival, which meant that he was given the pulpit to preach the afternoon sermon on Sunday and then a sermon every night of the following week. The parishioners and their guests were expected to attend church services throughout the week. It was during this week that many people "got religion." Getting religion was different for everyone. Some got it with great emotion—singing, screaming, or shouting—whereas others got it quietly.

The baptismal ceremony was one of the most important rites of passage in our community. All churches had what was called a "mourner's bench," which was usually the first pew in the church. When it was time for you to be baptized, you were expected to sit on the mourner's bench for however long it took to feel the spirit. How well I remember sitting on that bench. I didn't have the patience to wait, so I got religion pretty quickly, even though I never actually experienced that special feeling. All I knew was that I wanted to get the heck off the bench, the sooner the better.

After a couple of nights of sitting and waiting, I just got up one day, approached the pastor, shook his hand, and announced that I was ready to be baptized. He asked me questions like "Do you believe in Jesus Christ?" and "Are you willing to live a Christian life?" I answered appropriately and was baptized at the age of twelve.

Wearing a long white robe and accompanied by a deacon on each side of me, I approached the baptismal font, which was a swampy pond in the woods. The minister, dressed all in black and wading in waist-deep water, raised his hand and recited something from Scripture. Then he and one of the deacons laid hands on my head, instructed me to hold my breath, and dunked me in the water. As I was going down for the count, my thoughts were anything but spiritual. I said to myself, *I sure hope the water is not cold, and most of all, I sure hope I don't see a snake.* I had heard adults talk about having seen snakes along the swampy bank. Many of us were baptized that day, and after each candidate was submerged, the minister, the deacons, and the congregation broke out into song, "Wade in the Water."

At the time I was baptized, I had a childish concept of God and took my faith for granted. I thought that God would watch over me simply because I was part of the flock. It was only after I left home with the hope of making a better life for myself that I began to understand that I had to meet God halfway. I had to ask God to watch over me and give me guidance, strength, and courage. When I finally understood that it was up to me to open my heart, I began to draw on an inner strength that would help me find my way.

My spiritual growth didn't come easily. As with everything else in my life, I had to figure it out for myself. However, once I understood the connection between God and me, I knew one thing for sure: God would never abandon me, even if I strayed. I learned how to strengthen my faith through prayer and heed the words of Isaiah 48:17: "I am the Lord your God, who teaches you what is best for you, who directs you in the way you should go."

2

Fifth Avenue on a Wing and a Prayer

The first step toward success is taken when you refuse to be a captive of the environment in which you first find yourself.

—Mark Caine

School was over forever, or so it seemed. I was ready to make a life for myself away from the farm. My head was full of big-girl city dreams of making lots of money, meeting Prince Charming, and living happily ever after. I had living proof that such dreams—however clichéd—do come true. I just had to look at my relatives who had moved to New York. Looking the picture of success, they all had one thing in common: New York City. The Big Apple was the promised land, and I was going there to claim my fortune.

Mama had a different dream, however. Because I was her youngest child, she wanted nothing more than for me to go to college. She had every right to be disappointed with my desire to go to New York City. She was hoping that I would follow in her footsteps and go to her alma mater.

Unfortunately, we never sat down as mother and daughter to have a heart-to-heart talk about college or, for that matter, about how my mother, one of ten children, managed to put herself through college. It's mind-boggling to think that a poor southern black woman could have achieved such a goal, given the era in which she lived. It's an unsolved mystery in our family, like the eighth wonder of the world. The only reference my mother would make about college was in the form of an exhortation: "Lillian, if you stay home, maybe we can find a way for you to go to college." She uttered these thoughts with a painful longing, but I think she felt powerless. I simply wasn't interested in going to college. Besides, there was no money to pay for it, and it never occurred to either of us that scholarships and loans were available. We assumed that I had missed my one and only chance of a scholarship when the valedictorian and salutatorian of my high school received the two scholarships to Mama's alma mater. I was third in my class, so I missed my opportunity. I was disappointed, of course, but I wasn't devastated, because I was New York City bound. Everyone knew that life was better up North. At eighteen years old, an adult, I was perfectly capable of making my own decisions.

The only reason my parents agreed to let their young daughter leave home and travel so far away with nothing but a shell of a plan and no meaningful direction in life was that they knew I would be under the watch of family members. Much like the Underground Railroad of our ancestors, our family roots extended from Virginia as far north as Riverhead, New York, and New York City. In fact, with the help of my half brother, Henry, who lived in Riverhead, I already had a job waiting for me at an exclusive resort in Westhampton Beach, Long Island.

My parents squeezed out what comfort they could from knowing that at least I would not be on the streets like a vagabond. The plan was that my brother Weldon would pick me up in New Jersey, where he lived, and drive me to Henry's place in Riverhead. Henry would then drive me to the resort, where I would meet up with three of my high school classmates, who also had jobs waiting for them at the resort. The only positions open to black girls were in housekeeping, so we would be maids. Our consolation was that at least we had jobs.

To say that my departure was sad would be an understatement. With heavy hearts, my parents drove me to Netherland's country store and put me on the bus to Richmond en route to New Jersey. I had never seen my mother look so crestfallen. It was as if she thought she'd never see me again. Even Pa looked long-faced. We hugged and said good-bye. I was teary-eyed as I boarded the bus, already feeling melancholy and a bit worried. I began to wonder, *What if things don't work out? Could I go back home? If so, what would I do?* At that moment, this big girl didn't feel so big.

The resort in Westhampton Beach was something else; it exuded an elegance that we could look at but not touch. My girl-friends and I were immediately shown to our living quarters— a dormitory-style, wooden structure that looked like a cheap motel. Thank God we all shared a room. Otherwise, it might have been a strange, lonely, and disappointing summer. It didn't take us long to discover that Riverhead, which was where we hung out on our days off, was barely a step above Ballsville. It had a down-town area with streetlights, a department store, a few specialty shops, and a bank, as well as one main highway, Main Street.

The real problem with working in Westhampton Beach was the lack of public transportation to Riverhead. The resort was a distance from downtown Riverhead, much too far to walk. Although we could have walked to the town of Westhampton Beach, we didn't feel comfortable strolling around in a lily-white resort town. So on our days off, we depended on our relatives to drive us to Riverhead, which was where most of the resort's employees lived.

I admit that my summer would have been dreadful if I hadn't gotten my first taste of romance. The cliché about women fall-ing for men in uniforms held true for me because I fell for an air force man who was stationed at Westhampton Air Force Base. Like most teenage girls, I can still remember the name of my first love. Roger was about six feet tall, a bit heavy, and fair-skinned with smooth black hair. What I liked most about him was that he did not behave the way that I *imagined* city boys behaved, even though he had grown up in the Bronx. Of course, I didn't really know how city boys behaved, but I pictured them to be wild party types who saw themselves as God's gift to women.

The young man I met that summer was a real gentleman. He was quiet and soft spoken and had impeccable manners. It was also a plus that he had a car and a job. That summer proved to be quite a fun adventure, for I ignored my father's strict rules about dating and instead reveled in my newfound freedom. It was such a thrill when my boyfriend picked me up from work and took me to the movies, out to eat, or simply drove me around town. This was life at its best—at least until the end of summer when we were all at a crossroads.

Although my girlfriends and I made a decision to stay in New York State and seek better-paying jobs, they decided to remain on Long Island. I, on the other hand, stuck to my original plan to go to New York City. The hardest part of leaving Long Island was saying good-bye to my boyfriend, but he was becoming too serious for me. At nineteen years old, he had marriage on his mind, a notion that I wouldn't even consider at such a young age. So I left my summer job, my summer love, and my summer friends and went on my way to New York City.

Although I had a discussion with my parents about the possibility of my moving in with Hattie, who was now living in New York City, Hattie squelched the idea when she said her apartment was too small to accommodate me, especially since she was expecting her second child later that year. So I turned to plan B, which was to move in with my cousin Rema DePass. This was fine in theory, but it turned out that the living situation wasn't exactly what I expected. When I arrived, I found out that we would be sharing the apartment with her brother, Rudy. So much for spacious living. Little did I know the influence that Rudy would have in changing the course of my life.

At the time of my arrival, however, I wasn't ready to heed Rudy's counsel. It would take the school of hard knocks for me to listen to him about the importance of furthering my education. That came much later. For now, we were the three musketeers cramped into a one-bedroom apartment the size of a shoe box in the heart of Harlem.

To this day I wonder how we survived our living conditions. A long dark hallway led to a tiny living room, which led to the small bedroom where Rema and I slept. Rudy was relegated to sleeping on the living room sofa. I have to congratulate Rema for her ingenuity: the bedroom was not large enough to fit a double bed and a dresser, yet somehow she managed to squeeze everything in. We shared the bed, which was jammed against the wall, and the only way I could get to my side was to crawl across it. This was not the most convenient arrangement, especially when she was asleep and I had to crawl over her in the dark.

I finally adjusted to our cramped living space, but I never did adjust to the cockroaches in the kitchen. This was the first time that I had seen such nasty-looking critters, which inhabited our place as if they were rent-paying tenants. No matter how hard we tried, we couldn't get rid of them.

To put it bluntly, New York City was a shock to my system. Within days, I was overwhelmed by disappointment. The buildings were too tall, the streets too dirty, the city too crowded, and the people too cold. Gone were my visions of an exciting adventure: I felt lost, and for the first time I longed for the security and comfort of country living.

However, going home was not an option. There was no work for me there, and my parents would certainly not allow me to remain at home unemployed. Even if they would have let me do so, the farm would have driven me crazy. Instead, I made a decision: to stay and tough it out. It was time for Lillian to get real, and I had plenty to get real about, including my "get rich" fantasy.

Although I thought I was well prepared to land a decent-paying job as I was armed with a high school diploma and good typing skills, I soon discovered that there were few jobs for a hopeful, wide-eyed black girl in New York City. Nonetheless, I repeated a mantra that had been instilled in me by my mother: *I can do whatever I want to do if I want it badly enough.* All I really wanted, at that point, was a job. Mustering up reserves of resolve, which I didn't know I possessed, I applied for various office jobs, but I was always turned down. With my money running out and my patience running thin, I finally resigned myself to the one job I knew that I could get: I would become a domestic.

Swallowing my pride, I began working for a family on Fifth Avenue. I was not long for this job, however, and I reminded myself every day that I didn't leave home to become a maid in Manhattan. In the meantime, I was determined to glean something instructive or useful from this experience, no matter how bad it was. I justified my work as a maid by telling myself that at least I was being exposed to the way the wealthy lived. And I liked what I saw: a well-appointed, well-furnished apartment with fancy appliances, closets full of clothes, and servants tending to the family's needs. This was the kind of life I aspired to, even though I had no idea how I was going to get there. But one thing I knew for sure: I wasn't going to get very far if I continued with this line of work.

My circumstances forced me to a level of introspection that I had never experienced before, and I became obsessed with how to improve my status in life, how to earn money, and how to make it in the world. I was more determined than ever to use everything I possessed—wits, intelligence, stamina, and courage—to find my way. That's when I began to look at my life more creatively. Rema worked at Macy's department store on 34th Street, and she suggested that I apply for a job there. It sounded like an excellent idea. Taking a day off from my maid's job, I dressed that morning as professionally as I knew how, wearing the only suit I owned and my only pair of high heels.

How well I remember that day in October 1958. I had never been to Macy's, nor had I ever seen a store as large. As I came up the subway stairs, I was awestruck. There before me was a massive building that occupied an entire block. My only point of reference was Richmond's department stores, Thalhimer's and Miller & Rhoads, but these two combined would not take up an entire New York City block. Before I knew it, I was already fantasizing about how it would feel to work there, the people I would meet and the shopping I would do.

My mind was filling up with visions of the good life, but reality soon set in. When I approached the employment office and told the woman behind the desk that I wanted to apply for a job, the first words out of her mouth were, "Do you have work experience?" I replied, "No," answering the way I was brought up—to be honest. Besides, I didn't think it would make any difference whether I had experience since I had my high school diploma and excellent typing skills. She replied, "We only hire people with experience." That day I hit rock bottom. Disillusioned, I returned to my maid's job.

Nevertheless, I was not ready to settle for rejection. The Christmas season was approaching, and I was convinced that Macy's would hire me as a seasonal employee even if I didn't have any work experience. Again I went to the employment office, and I was asked the same question: "Do you have work experience?" Again I answered, "No." The result was the same: I was turned down. This time when I left Macy's, I was furious but even more determined to get a job there, and get it soon.

When I'm told I can't do something that I know I'm capable of doing, I summon a higher power. The time had come for a "come to Jesus" meeting with myself: I had to be my own advocate, to give this country girl with big dreams the opportunity she deserved. Over the next few days, I carefully thought about how to land a Macy's job. It was obvious that what was getting in my way was lack of experience.

That's when an idea occurred to me. I thought, *Why not create some work experience?* I was treading on dangerous ground, but I had to do what I had to do. I knew that on my return to Macy's employment office that I had to be armed with fictitious company names, including made-up names of supervisors and telephone numbers. Although I wasn't proud of myself for devising this scheme, I was at least pleased to have come up with what seemed to be a workable solution: I reasoned that it was less risky to provide fake employment names than to give real names.

My plan was hatched. I tried out several fictitious names in my head repeatedly until one caught my fancy and sounded legitimate. Then I envisioned myself at the office, role-playing how it would feel to be standing in front of the hiring supervisor and looking confident when she asked me the you-know-what question. I instinctively knew that people who are not telling the truth often give themselves away with their body language, so I wanted to make sure that when I approached my "adversary" (which is how I viewed the situation), I would have the countenance that would convince the hiring person that I had worked for those companies. I thought back to my high school days and how I loved to act in plays. I was now getting ready to put my acting skills to good use once again.

After waiting a few weeks, I returned to Macy's for the third time. I thought it was important to have some time elapse between interviews because I didn't want to be recognized as the young woman who had been rejected (twice). This time, when the employment officer asked the question "Do you have work experience?" I responded with a resounding "Yes."

Much to my surprise (although I didn't dare show it), I was then asked to complete a job application. Under the "previous employment" section, I carefully wrote down the names of three fake companies with Richmond, Virginia, addresses. After I handed in my application, I was given a typing test. I waited nervously for the results, thinking that this could be either the beginning or the end for me. After reviewing the application and grading the typing test, the hiring lady came back to the waiting room where I was sitting. She looked pale and confused and was barely able to get her words out as she said, "You did so well on the test, I'm not sure we can afford to hire you." I thought, *Lady, if you only knew what I had to do to get this job, you wouldn't hire me!* I just smiled.

As a devout Baptist whose life had always revolved around church, I felt guilty for telling this "little white lie," but I also knew that this was the only way I would be given the chance to prove my worth. I rationalized that my lie was not immoral when put in the context of wanting to better my lot in life. I thought that even God would approve of such a worthy cause. I was also willing to live with the consequences of my action if I were to be found out.

My gamble paid off. The good Lord must have wanted me to get this job because Macy's never checked my references. I was offered a job, earning forty-five dollars a week as a clerk-typist in the comparison shopping department. This was more money than I could ever have imagined. I savored my first taste of success in New York City.

* * *

My work environment at Macy's was pleasant enough, and I certainly had no complaints about how I was treated by my supervisor, an older white woman who had been a Macy's employee for many years. After a year, however, the thrill was gone. I just couldn't survive on my salary. After taxes were withheld and I had paid for rent, utilities, food, and transportation, I had nothing left. By payday, I was usually down to my last dime. In fact, I needed my paycheck before I could buy lunch and pay subway fare home that day.

My plan to become the owner of more than one pair of shoes had to be shelved. I've always loved shoes, but I couldn't seem to afford to buy more than one pair at a time. By the time I had enough money to buy a second pair, the first pair had completely worn out. However, I vowed that someday, when I could afford it, I would buy as many pairs of shoes as my heart desired. I kept that promise, and as soon as I could afford it, I bought shoes whether or not I needed them. To this day, I often admire my closetful of shoes—smart but comfortable shoes, like those from Cole Haan and Stuart Weitzman.

At the same time that I was getting tired of my Macy's job, Rudy started talking to me about why I should go to college. Rudy was a college graduate who had gone to my mother's alma mater. However, I still wasn't ready to listen to him. To be perfectly blunt, I thought he was a nag. All I could think was, *How on earth does he think I can pay for college when I can barely meet my daily living expenses?* Still, my life wasn't going according to my plan since I had arrived in New York. In fact, I was spiraling downward like water circling a drain. In addition to my deteriorating financial situation, I was not having any luck meeting people my age.

Only in retrospect did it occur to me that had I belonged to a church in those early days of living in the city, I might have met some young people who shared my interests. Furthermore, I'm sure that a church community would have kept me on the straight and narrow. Instead, I fell into the proverbial trap of the moral decrepitude of city life and the material world of wanting and obtaining.

Having left my soul and spiritual center back in Ballsville, I spent most of my free time with Rema (who was twelve years my senior), her friends, and an older uncle. We'd all end up at our apartment, have a few drinks, and gamble, playing poker and another card game called tonk. I really got hooked on tonk, and even though I was a pretty good card player, I still ended up burning a hole in my pocketbook, which worsened my financial condition. I began to feel guilty and ashamed, knowing how terrible my parents would feel if they knew I was involved in something they would consider the devil's work. God knows what could have happened to me had I continued down this path, but fortunately I do not have an addictive personality. As soon as I saw the financial hole I was digging myself into, I put an end to my gambling days.

Not only was I dissatisfied with my job, I was also very unhappy with my living arrangement. That's when I thought about my cousin Shirley, who had moved to Jamaica, New York. She had been trying for a very long time to get me to move in with her. I wanted to live with her, but I didn't want to go back to doing domestic work, which was what she was doing and what I would most likely have to do. I finally relented when she told me that she was making between fifteen and twenty dollars a day, which was a lot more than my nine-dollars-a-day paycheck from Macy's. It was an obvious decision.

To my surprise, my new environment was a welcome change from the crowded streets of New York City. Shirley and I shared a basement apartment in a private home in suburbia, and I liked it a lot. The owners treated us like family. They invited us to share meals and included us in many social activities and family gatherings. We also had a male cousin who lived in Jamaica, and he had a car. Shirley and I came up with a satisfying quid pro quo. He agreed to drive us wherever we asked him to take us—the grocery store, parties, or the subway station—and we agreed to cook for him.

Although I had the potential of making more money as a maid than I had been making at Macy's, I had to first build up my client base, which was proving to be difficult and time-consuming. Even though I managed to land one client, I continued to scan the newspapers for another line of work. I was really sick and tired of job hunting.

It's funny how life plays little tricks on you, perhaps as a way of keeping you humble. Had I known then what I learned later about how lucrative the cleaning business was, perhaps I would have had a different attitude and approached my maid job differently. I often laugh at myself when I think about how the job I hated so much early in life ended up being the basis of a successful business more than fifteen years later.

One day I was looking for a distraction, and I found a doozy. I became involved in one of the oldest flimflams in the world. As I was walking down Jamaica Avenue, oblivious to the world, I was approached by a young man who was ranting and raving about how he had just found some money. He excitedly explained that he was willing to share his newfound wealth with me if I would just show "good faith" by proving that I had money in the bank.

This was absurd because I did not have one cent in the bank. Nonetheless, I decided to play his game. I was bored with my life and therefore vulnerable. As he described the game plan, I thought, *This guy must think I am crazy.* As naive as I was at the age of nineteen, I was still smart enough to know that no one was going to give me money without expecting something in return.

I detected a bit of danger in the air but rationalized it away, thinking, *What could happen to me in broad daylight?* So instead of walking away, I walked alongside him. Spotting a bank up ahead—not my bank, just a bank on the street—I indicated to this scam artist that I was willing to make a withdrawal. I asked him to wait outside the bank while I went inside, and I pretended to go up to the counter to withdraw some money.

When I came out of the bank, he wanted to see the money. I stalled by telling him to wait until we got out of the flow of traffic. The game was getting a little dicey at this point, and I had to think fast. I started to pick up my pace, and after a few blocks I turned to him and broke the news that I had changed my mind and would not give him the money. Then I ran down the street like a bat out of hell.

Looking back to make sure that he wasn't following me, I noticed that he was frozen in space, dumbfounded. I'm sure he thought that I would be an easy target, but instead I scammed him. Later that evening, when I told Shirley about my escapade, she looked at me in horror, exclaiming, "Are you crazy?" I just laughed and said, "Of course not. It was fun." I did not share with her how scared I had been. Years later, I learned that many innocent and naive people have lost much of their life savings falling for this get-rich-quick scheme.

That October (1960) as I was scouring the help-wanted section of the newspaper, my eyes fell on an ad that read "Make money and travel." The travel part piqued my interest because I was longing for an adventure. I went for an interview, and the recruiter, a white guy in his mid-thirties, painted a glamorous picture, describing how I would be traveling around the country selling magazine subscriptions.

What really got my attention, however, was when he said that I would be earning points toward a college scholarship. Suddenly this job was beginning to sound very intriguing. Since I wasn't getting very far with my school-of-hard-knocks degree, college was looking better and better. If this sounded too good to be true, that's because it was, but again I had to learn the hard way.

Without further ado, I accepted the offer on the spot. My first mistake was not asking questions that would have helped me make an informed decision. For example, I didn't ask where we would be traveling, how I would earn scholarship points, how many points I would earn for making a sale, and what evidence I would receive that I had earned scholarship points. These were basic questions, but I acted impulsively.

Up to this point, my mother had refrained from commenting on or criticizing my choice of jobs because at least she knew that I was living in one place and that family was always close by. However, when I told her that my new job required that I travel around the country, she expressed concern. I set off an alarm in her head when I told her that I would be traveling with a group of white kids.

For the first time since I had moved to New York City, my mother erupted into a full-blown lecture about my safety and the undertow of discrimination. She warned me that even though prejudice wasn't as obvious in the North as it was in the South, racial discrimination was everywhere. Speaking with the passion of a preacher, she exclaimed that it just wasn't safe for a black girl to be on the streets by herself, going door-to-door selling magazines. But as hard as she tried to dissuade me, I refused to listen. Unfortunately, as my mother knew all too well, once I made up my mind, no one could change it.

Was I in for a rude awakening. The job was a disaster right from the start. Going to places like inner-city Philadelphia and Washington, D.C., wasn't exactly my idea of traveling the country. The scholarship money was also a fraud. The only thing that impressed me about the organization was that it knew how to pick clean-cut, naive, and trusting young adults. What was most fascinating about this outfit was that its victims were mostly poor whites. I was thrown into the mix for the simple reason that the company could use me to expand its reach into black neighborhoods.

I'll never forget my first night on the job. We were taken to a cheap hotel in Manhattan where we spent the night before heading south early the next morning. There was a quick training program that night in which we learned the drill and our sales pitch. The sales pitch was key because we were told that it was a surefire way to close the sale. How could an adult with any conscience slam the door on a poor, ambitious, and earnest kid who was selling magazine subscriptions as a way of earning a scholarship to go to college? This was the stuff of the American Dream.

Our first stop was Newark, New Jersey, followed by Philadelphia, Baltimore, and Washington, D.C. We were given a quota for the number of subscriptions to sell with a warning that if we didn't meet our quota by the scheduled pickup time in the late afternoon, we'd be sent right back out that evening, until we did meet it. The real incentive for meeting the quota was more about survival than earning points toward a scholarship. We knew that if we didn't meet our targets that we'd be sent back into the streets *without dinner.* That was too cruel for words.

My sales pitch worked like a charm on my clientele. I was always well received, and I loved to watch people's faces light up when I told them that I was trying to earn a college scholarship. There's nothing more exciting to black people than to hear that one of their own is going to college. They couldn't subscribe fast enough, which meant that I seldom failed to meet my quota.

On the few occasions that I did fail, I managed to talk my way out of going back out at night by telling my supervisor that I didn't feel safe being out alone after dark. For some reason, he let me off the hook. This wasn't the case for another young lady in the group, for whom I felt sorry. Rarely meeting her quota, she was always sent back into the streets and sometimes didn't return until ten o'clock at night. It seemed that she couldn't do anything right; the supervisor was always picking on her.

In the beginning, I was hopeful about earning my points for a scholarship. But after several weeks passed, I asked my supervisor about the points. He assured me that I would be receiving a report at the end of the month. The pay was meager, but I wasn't concerned about it then because I was getting free room and board, and besides, I thought I was accumulating scholarship points.

In early December, when I hadn't yet received my monthly report, I approached my supervisor again. All he said was that it was coming. That's when I began to question what was going on. How hard was it to produce a report? Being competitive by nature, I was losing interest in selling because I didn't know how well I was doing. I also began to question the program and its claims, even to the point of wondering if the people who had subscribed to the magazines were actually receiving them. The longer I stayed with the organization, the worse I was feeling. I wanted to get out, but I had no money and no place to go.

Christmas was approaching. It was the first Christmas that I was away from home, and it was the worst Christmas that I have ever had, before that time and since. I was used to being with my family, sitting around the Christmas tree, eating, opening gifts, and spreading good cheer. Now I was stuck in a hotel in Washington, D.C., that felt more like an orphanage. We were a sorry lot: poor, sad, homeless-looking kids.

Although the manager tried to make the holidays as pleasant as possible by arranging a company-sponsored Christmas dinner for us at the hotel, it didn't help my spirits. I sank so low that night and I knew I couldn't last another day. The next day, I went to my manager and informed him that I was leaving. He must have seen the determination in my eyes because he knew that this time he couldn't change my mind. There had been a few occasions in which he had successfully talked me out of leaving by telling me that I was his top salesperson and that he didn't want to lose me.

Once he realized that this time I wouldn't waver, he accepted my decision and even offered to drive me to the Greyhound bus station. He bought my ticket to Virginia and put me on the bus. I'll never know whether his gesture was genuine or whether he just wanted to get rid of me because he didn't want to take any chances that I would express my concerns and suspicions to my colleagues and perhaps instigate a riot. Later in my life, when young people would approach me with the same scholarship sales pitch, I tried my best to convince them that they were being used by the company. I can only hope that my words of caution made a difference in someone's life.

I wasn't looking forward to the long, dreary trip from D.C., but it would give me time to think. I was going home with mixed feelings. Although I was eager to see my family, I was concerned about how I would be received. Would my family think that I was a failure?

My fears were for naught. The Greyhound bus came to a stop on the main highway just in front of Aunt Alberta's convenience store. When I looked out the bus window, there was my entire family standing outside the store, smiling and waving at me. (My sister and my brothers were there, having come home for Christmas.) I was touched beyond words. We hugged one another and cried. I had never felt as much love as I did at that moment. When we arrived home, no one ever said "I told you so" or scolded me for making stupid decisions. For a few days, I relaxed with my family and put my future on hold. I was safe and sound.

3

In the Company of Angels

It is this belief in a power larger than myself and other than myself which allows me to venture in the unknown and even the unknowable.

—Maya Angelou

With one piercing question, my mother snapped me out of the confused state that I had been in since I returned home: "What are your plans, Lillian?" she asked. All I could say was, "I don't know." Clyde and Weldon, who were still home for the holidays, overheard our conversation. Weldon took this as a cue, sashayed into the dining room with a comb in his hand—he was forever combing his hair—and chimed in, "Lillian, why don't you come back to New Jersey with us and try to find a job?"

The look on Mom's face told us how she felt about this idea. I'm sure she was concerned that my brothers were single and that this might not be an appropriate environment for a young woman. In a split second, however, her expression changed, as if the sun had just radiated through a storm cloud. She must have flashed back to my last job as a traveling saleswoman, because suddenly Weldon's proposal seemed like a good plan. At least she knew that my brothers would be there to protect me.

On the day we left for New Jersey, we decided to drop by to say good-bye to my aunt Alberta, who lived in Powhatan. Alberta was quite a character, and I loved being around her. When I was in high school, I couldn't wait to spend weekends with her. She and her husband owned a convenience store, which was unusual for blacks in those days. Harris's Esso & Grocery Store teemed with activity and entertainment, which was a pleasant change from the quiet of my home life. The atmosphere was always upbeat, with people coming in and out of the store in a breezy sort of way.

Harris's was more than a convenience store. It had a clubby feel, with an open floor space, a jukebox, and booths along the wall. The patrons would typically purchase snacks and soft drinks and sit in the booths and socialize. The open space served as a dance floor. I'd love to hear people drop coins into the jukebox and select their favorite tunes. One song that usually got folks dancing was "Let the Good Times Roll" by Shirley & Lee.

I especially enjoyed being around Alberta, who was as fun loving as she was enterprising. Most of all, she was a smart, fashionable dresser and a looker who always had her makeup just so and her hair perfectly coiffed. She gave me one piece of advice that I follow to this day: "Never go to bed with your makeup on. It ruins your skin."

The day we dropped by to say good-bye, Alberta was full of questions about my plans to go to New Jersey. She came at me like a cat burrowing into a paper bag looking for catnip. She asked, "Why New Jersey?" When I told her that I had no place else to go, she replied, "Why not go to Washington, D.C.?" I was shocked by such an outrageous idea because I knew absolutely no one there.

Alberta obviously had something up her sleeve. In an efficient and authoritative manner, she picked up the phone right then and there and called an old friend who lived in Washington. I was not privy to the conversation because she made the call from a phone booth that was tucked into a corner of the store. After the call, Alberta informed me that she had made arrangements for me to stay with her friend in D.C.

The next phone call she made was to my mother to tell her of the change in plans. Mama must have approved because before I knew what hit me, my brothers were driving me to Washington,

D.C. Before we left, Alberta told me all about her friend, Marie Trent, including that she was a native of Powhatan and had lived there long before I was born.

As we approached Marie Trent's home in the northeast part of the city, I was struck by how neat and tidy the neighborhood looked. It reminded me of the neighborhood where I had lived in Jamaica, New York. The streets were clean, the sidewalks were paved, and single-family houses were lined up in a neat row like soldiers in the line of duty. Marie's home was different from most of the other houses in the neighborhood. It was a lovely, stand-alone brick bungalow that sat on a slight hill and looked more modern than the row houses that surrounded it. We arrived two days before the New Year, and one look at this neighborhood gave me a good feeling. I felt in my bones that 1961 was going to be a very good year.

My hunch was confirmed when I met Marie Trent, who was a quiet, unassuming woman in her mid-forties. She welcomed me with open arms, which spoke volumes, considering that she was taking in a stranger on such short notice. When our conversation turned to the rent, her loving and compassionate nature wafted over me like a summer breeze. She simply said, "Don't worry about it. Let's talk about that later." Any discomfort that I had about not having a job, much less any money, was immediately dispelled by her kind words. Over time, I would come to think of Marie not only as my adopted mother but also as a saint.

I was excited to meet the Trent household, which I would soon learn was a lively assortment of people, consisting of Marie's two teenagers—a son and a daughter—a daughter about five years old, and her deceased husband's nephew, who was about thirty years old. I was impressed when she told me that her nephew worked full time during the day and attended Howard University at night.

Inside this house full of love were four bedrooms: Marie and her eldest daughter each had a bedroom, her son and her nephew shared a bedroom, and I shared a room with the five-year-old, who saw me as her new playmate. A special bond developed between Darlene and me. She was the little sister I never had, and I used to love to read to her as she sat on my lap, hanging on to my every word and squeezing me tightly.

As I said, Marie was a saint, and I give her credit for rekindling my spiritual life. On the first Sunday in my new home, she invited me to go with her family to her Baptist church. It had been a long time since I had attended a Sunday service, but the minute the doors of the church swung open, my heart softened and my soul filled with Bible verses and familiar hymns from my childhood. A passage that I had heard as a child but never really understood suddenly had meaning: "Train a child in the way he should go, and when he is old he will not turn from it." As I reflected on my years in New York City, I realized that only God could have helped me survive some of the challenges I had faced there. Sitting in the pew that first Sunday in Marie Trent's church, I promised myself that no matter where I lived, I would not only become actively involved in a church community, but I would also forge an unbreakable bond with my Lord all the days of my life. After a few visits, I joined the church and, shortly thereafter, the choir. To this day I sing in my church choir.

*   *   *

How well I remember January 1961. John F. Kennedy was sworn in as president on January 20, a cold wintry day. By noon, Washington, D.C., was covered with eight inches of snow, which was considered blizzard conditions in a city that was not used to dealing with much snow. Nothing, however, was going to put a damper on the inauguration ceremony. Army flamethrowers were out in force clearing the snow from Pennsylvania Avenue. Although I was glad to be a witness to this historic moment, I was also concerned about all the snow. I was worried that it would interfere with my job search, which had to begin the very next day, snow or no snow.

The election of Kennedy was a curious phenomenon that resulted in an unlikely split in the Hobson household. Like most other families we knew, my parents were registered Democrats, but my parents disagreed over the worth of this dark horse. It was the first—and the last—time that my mother and father would cancel each other's vote. My father did not hesitate to cast his vote for Kennedy, but my mother voted for Richard Nixon because she was deeply troubled about having a Catholic in the White House. Her fear was that Kennedy would impose his religious beliefs on the American people, and this made her uncomfortable.

Mom, who took her voting rights as seriously as the air she breathed, was the only one in our neighborhood who had such a negative reaction to this man. She worked at the polls for the Democratic Party on Election Day, and I don't know how she justified her action, but she was a proud and righteous lady. Needless to say, it was one of the few decisions my mother lived to regret. She came to respect this president, even though he was Catholic, for all the good work he did to advance civil rights.

Washington, D.C., proved to be fertile ground for my job search, and I soon hit the jackpot. Browsing through the *Washington Post*'s help-wanted section, I came across a listing for a typist at a synagogue. The very next day I rode the bus to the synagogue, applied for the job, and was hired, with instructions to start the next day. I thought back to my New York City job-hunting days and couldn't believe my good fortune in being hired so quickly. I'm sure my experience at Macy's stood me in good stead. Having experience paid off, after all. The next morning I woke up extra early to make sure that I wouldn't be late for my first day on the job. I was in a really good mood and found myself singing all the way to the bus stop.

The job was an easy mix of basic typing and clerical work—not very exciting and not very challenging—but it was a job. At the end of the day, I hopped on the bus to go home. As I thought about my day, I felt a pleasant but vague daydreaming feeling come over me, until I suddenly realized that the bus ride seemed unusually long. I looked down at my watch, and reality hit me between the eyes: I had been on the bus for an hour and a half. I don't know whether it was because of the excitement of landing a job so early in my search that the length of my commute did not register before now, but I couldn't believe how long I was on the bus and how long a bus ride I would have to endure to get to and from work every day. The synagogue was located all the way across town in the upper northwest section of the city. When I thought about the three-hour round-trip commute, I knew immediately that the job was not right for me. I made up my mind on the bus ride home that afternoon. I called my boss in the morning and explained that I wouldn't be returning because the commute was too long.

Again, Marie came to my rescue. When I informed her of my decision, she immediately suggested that I take the civil service exam. Being new to the city, I had no idea what the exam was all about, but it sounded like a good idea. After all, I thought, Washington, D.C., is a government town, so many of its residents work for the federal government. Marie gave me the necessary information, and I arranged to take the exam. When I was notified that I had passed the test and qualified at a grade 3 level, I was elated. My next assignment was to ascertain which agencies had job openings for a grade 3 typist.

It didn't take me long to find a job as a typist for the Veterans Administration in the Veteran Affairs division. My annual salary was just shy of $4,000, about $75 a week, which was much more than my previous salary at Macy's. On my first day, I made sure to arrive early to have enough time to find my office. Thank God I did. The Veterans Administration building occupied an entire block on Vermont Avenue and H Street NW. Just finding my way around the building was a challenge.

When I finally arrived at my destination, I was greeted by a supervisor who proceeded to show me to my desk in a room with about fifty people sitting at rows of desks with typewriters and Dictaphones. Without even giving me an introduction to the other workers, she explained in a clipped tone that I would be transcribing medical reports and that spelling and accuracy were critically important. She then ran through the drill as if she couldn't wait to be finished with me, telling me that after I completed a transcription I was to walk up to the front of the room and put it in a box.

Hanging on to every word, I took my seat and scanned the room for a glimpse of my colleagues. What I saw alarmed me. Everyone, except for one of the supervisors, was black; everyone seemed at least ten years older than I; and all were women except for two men. This was the first time in my short career that I questioned why the employees were mostly black people. Having worked up North, I was used to being a minority, so this job felt strange from that perspective.

I didn't have time to ponder this odd environment, however, because it was time to start typing. It didn't take long to discover that I was in over my head. Without medical training, I found the tapes difficult to decipher. Not only did the doctors mumble and talk fast, they also used medical terms that I could neither understand nor spell. Recalling the warning of my supervisor that all words had to be spelled correctly or else I would be penalized, I was at my wit's end.

To make matters worse, we did not have individual dictionaries at our desks. If it was necessary to look up a word, we had to get out of our seats and go to the front of the room to use the master dictionary. I struggled through the morning and managed to finish two reports. As I marched to the front of the room to drop my second transcription in the box, I looked around the room: everyone looked serious but confident. The rat-a-tat-tat of typewriters was the only sound. It was obvious that this was a no-nonsense workplace.

Then suddenly there was a stir in the room. As if on cue, everyone stopped typing, got up, and walked toward the door.

I glanced at my watch; it was exactly noon. When a woman passed by me, I asked her where everyone was going, and she told me it was lunchtime. Not wanting to miss lunch, I too headed for the door and was approached by two women who asked me to join them. Thank goodness for the kindness of strangers.

When we sat down for lunch, my new companions, Vivian Williams and Lois Patterson, gave me the lowdown on the typing pool, where both had been working for a couple of years. What they told me made me feel as if I had just enlisted in the army. You had to be at work at 8:00 a.m. not 8:01; otherwise you'd be docked fifteen minutes. Everyone went to lunch at noon and returned at 12:30 p.m. The workday ended at 4:30 p.m., and not one minute earlier. Even if you completed your work at 4:25 p.m., you had to sit at your desk until 4:30.

The litany of rules continued. There was a short break in the morning and another in the afternoon. When the transcriptions were dropped in the box, a supervisor would randomly select one to evaluate. If you had the misfortune of receiving a bad evaluation, you would be reprimanded for poor performance, and even worse, your raise could be affected. Listening to the lists of dos and don'ts, I knew it was going to be a doozy of a place. My only consolation was meeting these two friendly women, who welcomed me into their circle. At exactly 4:30 p.m. I left the office for my forty-five-minute bus ride home.

It was around this time that Marie's college-enrolled nephew who lived with us began inviting me to parties thrown by his Howard University classmates. I was suddenly introduced to a whole new class of people—college students. At one of the parties I remember thinking that college kids seemed to have lots of fun. Notice that I was thinking more about my social life than about the educational aspect.

Meanwhile, the job at the Veterans Administration was going reasonably well. I had adjusted to the rigors of the work environment, and the pay was okay. My performance was above average, which meant that whenever my work was pulled for review, I received a satisfactory evaluation. Most important, my relationship with Vivian developed into what would become a lifelong friendship. Over the years, our love for travel became a special bond between us, and we took many vacations together, including family vacations (once we both had families). Our friendship spanned forty-six beautiful years until she died suddenly of a heart attack in 2007.

Still, something was missing. Visions of the Fifth Avenue family were lingering in my mind, and I was growing increasingly dissatisfied with my station in life. Then one day, when Vivian and I were on our lunch break, I erupted like Mount Vesuvius and burst out, "Vivian, I can't take it anymore. I can't see myself doing this for the rest of my life. I have to find a way out."

She responded in a mature manner that reflected our eight-year age difference: "I understand, Lillian. What do you have in mind?" I answered, "I'm not sure, but I have to come up with something."

That's when I recalled one of the college parties I had gone to and how impressed I was when one of the young women told me that she was attending the District of Columbia Teachers College (now known as the University of the District of Columbia) on a part-time basis. She gave me oodles of information, and I remember how excited I was that night when I came home from the party. I could barely sleep, thinking about the possibility of going to college. As I put all my job experiences into perspective, I began to realize that I wasn't getting very far. It was the spring of 1961, and if I wanted to go to college in the fall, I had to act quickly.

I immediately obtained an admissions application for the District of Columbia Teachers College, filled it out, and was accepted as a part-time student for the fall semester. To think that this one decision was responsible for taking my life in a completely new direction is sobering.

I didn't know it at the time, but I later found out that Mom had been plotting with Rudy to convince me to go to college. She told him to keep talking to me about the necessity of getting a college education. I thought that he sounded like a broken record, when all along he was following my mother's precise instructions to make me understand the value of an education. My mother and Rudy were so delighted and relieved when I announced to them that I had finally enrolled as a part-time student in a college program. Their work was done, and Mama's lifetime goal was accomplished. Her prayers were answered.

Between working during the day and going to school at night, I was carrying a full load. My life was truly hectic. I went to school on Monday and Wednesday, leaving work at 4:30 p.m. to catch the bus for two evening classes that began at 6 p.m. and ended at 9 p.m. I arrived home an hour later and stayed up into the wee hours of the morning to study. The routine started all over again at 6 a.m., when I arose to get ready for work. The first semester went well. I enjoyed learning, and my grades were good. The following semester I upped the ante. I took nine hours of coursework, going to school Monday, Tuesday, Wednesday, and Thursday.

In the spring of 1962, a job opportunity with the Peace Corps came my way. This job would be a promotion, moving me from grade 3 to grade 4 in the civil service. I was hired by what turned out to be one of the most understanding and supportive supervisors I have ever had. The difference between working for Ruth DiMisa at the Peace Corps and working at the Veterans Administration was like night and day.

After entertaining a fleeting thought about going to Cameroon as a Peace Corps volunteer, I knew that I had to remain grounded and continue my studies. I'm glad I did, for it was at the Peace Corps that I met another lifelong friend, Anna Hart. Even though I was still only a clerk-typist, I found the Peace Corps work more interesting, thanks to Ruth, who made sure that Anna and I were given intellectually stimulating projects to type. Learning about various parts of the world was like giving a child free rein in a candy store. I relished every morsel of travel knowledge. Ruth did a lot more for Anna and me: she created a friendly, welcoming workplace. At last I had found a job that was a pleasure to go to every day.

Yet, even though the work was going well and my grades were good, I was finding it increasingly stressful to balance work and school. I reached the breaking point when my inner voice spelled out the reality I was facing: *Lillian, at this rate, you'll be an old lady by the time you finish college, and you can't keep up this pace.* It was then that I knew I had to find a way to become a full-time student.

One evening, on the bus ride home from my night class, I decided to seek help. I thought of good old Rudy, who was now living in Washington, D.C. I knew that he had gone to college full time, and he probably hadn't had much more money than I now had for tuition, so I wondered how he did it.

It's amazing what you learn when you're willing to open up to people and take them into your confidence. Rudy was more than happy—flattered, even—to tell me how to apply for financial aid. Following his advice, I applied to Howard University and at the same time applied for student loans and scholarships. I was elated when I heard that I was accepted and had received the necessary funds to enroll as a full-time student.

I had been at my job with the Peace Corps for only a few months when I was accepted at Howard, and I was reluctant to tell my supervisor that I was going to be leaving to go to school full time. I needn't have been concerned, however. Ruth was her usual understanding and helpful self. In fact, she offered to work out a suitable arrangement for me to continue to work at the Peace Corps part time. I had everything that I had hoped for: acceptance to college, a scholarship, a loan, and a part-time job at the Peace Corps.

I would learn from many experiences, but this chapter of my life taught me two of life's greatest lessons. First, our goals are not reached in a vacuum or without aid from others who want to help us to succeed. Second, asking for help is a sign of strength and intelligence, not a sign of weakness and lack of intelligence.

CHAPTER

4

Howard University and Lucky 13

*There weren't any MBAs that I knew about, and I had this
very strong conviction that if I could get a professional education
in the field of business, that is what I wanted. There wasn't any
question in my mind about what I wanted.*

—H. Naylor Fitzhugh, Harvard MBA (class of 1933)

The year is 1966. It's a glorious spring day, and the sun is shining brightly. Folding chairs are set up in neat rows across a freshly mowed lawn. I look up toward the sky and squint at the majestic clock tower rising above Howard University's Founders Library. My mind races back to that fateful day in November 1963, when the news broke that President Kennedy had just been shot, and I went running across the campus to the library with the fear of God in me to find out whether I had to report to my job that afternoon.

At the far end of campus, professors and administrators are dressed in caps and gowns and stand in formation, ready to begin the processional march to a makeshift stage. Hundreds of students follow. The air is electrifying; good cheer is everywhere. I'm one of the students in the procession. I pick out my family in a sea of smiling faces. My mother is looking straight at me, beaming with pride; my dad is sitting contentedly with his chest puffed

63

out; my siblings, cousins, nieces, and other relatives are engaged in lively conversations with one another.

I take a deep breath as I walk across the stage to receive my bachelor's degree. This must be a dream. Soon I'll wake up and find myself stuck in Ballsville. No, it's not a dream; this is my life unfolding.

*　　*　　*

I came to Howard University in the fall of 1962 at the age of twenty-two. Armed with my degree from the school of hard knocks, I found myself sitting with a bunch of seventeen- and eighteen-year-olds fresh out of high school. The difference in life experience and maturity between me and my fellow classmates was stunning, and the reality of being a full-time undergraduate student was even more stunning.

It was unfathomable to think that I had to sit through a one-hour, noncredit, two-semester required course called Freshman Assembly every Wednesday afternoon in the large auditorium in Ira Aldridge Hall. Orientation to college life was not what I needed because it was obvious to me why I was there: to get my college degree and get on with my life. I already had a head start: I was able to transfer twelve credits from the District of Columbia Teachers College.

As one of the larger historically black universities, Howard University sits on an idyllic campus on a hilltop on Georgia Avenue in northwest Washington, D.C. In fact, the student newspaper is called the *Hilltop* in honor of the university's breathtaking setting. This campus is quite a contrast to the University of the District of Columbia, which has no campus at all: it is a collection of institutional-looking buildings that sprawl along the streets not too far from Howard.

Founded in 1867 by Oliver O. Howard, a white Civil War hero known for promoting the welfare and education of former slaves, freedmen, and war refugees, Howard University has a rich history of providing educational opportunities to blacks when they were routinely denied access to white colleges and universities. It made me proud to add my name to the list of renowned black leaders, intelligentsia, and entertainers: Vernon Jordan, Douglas Wilder (the first black governor in the country, elected in Virginia in 1989), Edward Brooke (the first black U.S. senator elected in the twentieth century), Toni Morrison, Phylicia Rashad, and Roberta Flack, to name a few. One of the university's more highly acclaimed graduates, Thurgood Marshall, had been turned down for admission by the University of Maryland Law School.

Shortly after I arrived in D.C., I learned that I had a first cousin who lived in the city with his wife and her nephew. I visited them from time to time, and we all got along just fine. During one of my visits, my cousin and his wife suggested that I move in with them so that I could be closer to the university. I was still living with the Trents when I enrolled at Howard, and I couldn't have been happier with the arrangement, except for one thing—the commute to campus was about two hours round-trip. From my cousin's house, the commute would be only one hour. I was still considering their offer when they told me that I would have my own bedroom. Being closer to the campus and having the solitude and quiet to study sealed the deal. It was a sad day when I said good-bye to the Trents, who felt like family, but I promised to stay in touch.

My first semester course work was manageable, with the exception of physical science, a required course that I should have postponed taking until I had become acclimated to college life. The course was held in an area on campus called Death Valley, where all required courses for science majors were held. Death Valley was an appropriate name because the site was located down the hill from the main campus, in an actual valley, and the courses taught there were considered to be the most difficult. In fact, it was well known that this was the place where students dropped courses, changed majors, or did not survive the curriculum.

There I was, one of more than a hundred students sitting in a large auditorium, waiting for the professor, who had a reputation for being humorous but tough. The minute he opened the door, this funny character started talking as if he couldn't wait to dispense critical knowledge that was bubbling out of his head. The sight of him brought some comic relief to an otherwise dreadful course. He was about five feet eight inches tall and of medium build, and he seemed to have a Cheshire cat grin permanently attached to his face. His name was Professor Joseph (Joe) Paige.

I had never experienced a lecture-style course in which I had to take voluminous, hand-cramping notes. After weeks of copying long scientific formulas that he scribbled on the blackboard, most of which looked like hieroglyphics, I realized that I did not understand much of the material. My stomach churned with the mere thought of flunking a course in my first semester.

No matter how hard I studied that first semester, my physical science class continued to cause me more stress than I could bear. I was at the breaking point when I decided that I needed to talk to Professor Paige and explain that I was lost in his class. Much to my surprise, when I stopped by his office to make an appointment, I discovered that not only was he approachable but that he had a big, generous heart as well.

He waved me into his office. With no time to gather my thoughts, I explained that I was overwhelmed in his class, emphasizing that I had never taken such a difficult science course. The curriculum at Pocahontas High School had never included advanced physics. I must have sounded like a bleating sheep when I told him that I couldn't afford to flunk the course because he immediately came up with a proposal of how I could satisfy the course requirement. He explained that he would accept a project that illustrated a topic that we were studying in class, such as velocity, gravity, or sound. Not wanting to push my luck, I thanked him and backed out of his office, completely mystified about what kind of project would qualify.

I was wracking my brain when a lightbulb went off in my head. My cousin's wife's nephew was a smart guy who had a mind for mechanics and electronics. I consulted this eager and bright seventeen-year-old to get some ideas about what to do. He came up with a project in no time at all, suggesting that I put together a model radio. He proceeded to instruct me about what I needed to purchase: a model kit, wires, and various other electrical components. This young Einstein was actually much more excited about the project than I was. I was thankful because it was much more complex than I could ever have imagined. Nonetheless, between his genius and my following his instructions, we completed the project to our satisfaction.

I was a bundle of nerves the day of my presentation. Walking quickly into Professor Paige's office, I wasted no time running wires and antennae everywhere, like a mad scientist unable to contain the results of her experiment. Then I hooked up the radio and pushed the button: music began to float out. Bravo! A big smile appeared on the professor's face, and an even bigger smile appeared on my face. I could see from his reaction that my presentation would help my grade; at least, I was certain, it wouldn't hurt it. The only thing he said was, "You did a good job."

Nevertheless, my fears were not allayed because I still had to sweat out the rest of the semester taking copious notes, quizzes, and tests before I got my final grade. At the end of the semester, I remember walking apprehensively to Death Valley hoping that I would at least get a C. When I saw a B posted on the bulletin board next to my anonymous ID number, I was ecstatic. I had survived Death Valley.

I was less successful on the social front. As an older student, I was the proverbial odd person out. Call me a stick in the mud, but I didn't have time to party and socialize like most college-age students. I was either studying to get good grades or working to pay for my education. Since I lived off campus and worked a lot, I found it difficult to be involved in campus life. Much of my social life was still with my friend Vivian, who was always supportive and encouraging, or with the group I had met at parties before enrolling at Howard.

In the first semester of my freshman year, my classes were held in the morning, which allowed me to continue working at the Peace

Corps. In the second semester, however, my supervisor told me that the higher-ups had informed her that I could no longer work part-time. I knew that Ruth had done the best she could, presenting a convincing case to allow me to continue working, but in the end she had to let me go.

If you believe that everything happens for a reason, then the sudden end to my Peace Corps job happened for a good one. When I met the director of student placement, Marian Coombs, I knew that a higher power was hard at work. Mrs. Coombs took me under her wing for the rest of my time at Howard, always guiding me to good student job opportunities.

Mrs. Coombs set up my first interview with a man who was looking for a typist for his research reports. When I was told that he worked out of his home in an apartment building on 18th Street NW, I was apprehensive about being interviewed in the apartment of an older man who lived and worked alone, but I had to trust that Howard's placement office wouldn't put me in harm's way.

When I arrived at the interview, I was greeted by a tall, rake-thin white man who appeared to be in his late fifties or early sixties. The interview was short and concluded with my taking a simple typing test. Later that day, Mrs. Coombs informed me that I had been hired by the strange-looking man on 18th Street.

My initial impression of my new employer was confirmed. A research scientist, he was a bit eccentric. He worked incessantly, spoke very little, and drank black coffee continuously throughout the day; I never saw him eat any food. We got along quite well because neither of us was eager to engage in much conversation. We just wanted to finish the work. I worked for him for at least a year, two or three days a week for four hours a day.

While everything was going well on the school and job fronts, my once-perfect living situation turned into a nightmare. There was a growing conflict between my cousin and his wife that involved her nephew. The once-sweet boy who had helped me on my science project got mixed up with a bad crowd, and his aunt didn't know how to handle him. At the same time, she turned against me and started lodging complaints to my cousin that I was staying up too late and burning too much electricity. I felt sorry for my cousin, who was trying to defend me while keeping the peace with his wife. To make a long story short, my cousin and I agreed that it would be best if I found another place to live.

I decided that this was as good a time as any to explore living on campus. If nothing else, it would be a novel experience. I found a single room in a dormitory located a short distance from the main campus. But it didn't take long for me to realize that dorm life was not for me. Not only was it restrictive, it was downright oppressive. Having lived on my own for four years, I was annoyed by all the stupid rules and silly curfews. In those days, female students had to be in the dorm by 9 p.m. on weeknights and by 10 p.m. on weekends. No exceptions were made for an older student like me who was used to more freedom. The rules were the rules. Breaking curfew resulted in having to give up a weekend by staying in the dorm—the equivalent of being grounded. Because of a delinquent act I committed, I still owe the dorm mother a weekend.

One weekend in May, my friend Anna was having a party, so I requested a late curfew. I was given a one-hour extension, until 11 p.m. I thought, *What kind of grace period is that?* I wasn't fazed by it, however, because I had no intention to be back by that time: the party would just be getting into full swing at that hour. At 1 a.m., I snuck back into the dorm as quietly as I could, but I had to enter through a special door so the dorm mother would know of my late return time. Maybe the door squeaked so that she would be able to know when one of her girls broke the curfew.

The next morning I had to face the music of abusing my extended curfew. Since this happened near the end of the semester, my house mother gave me the option of paying back the time the following weekend or carrying it over to the next school year. Having already decided that I would not be returning to the dorm in the fall, I quickly agreed to carry the time over to the next year. At twenty-three years old, I could not tolerate living under such ridiculous rules.

I knew that I had to make alternative living arrangements for the fall, but it was now heading into summer and my mind was elsewhere. I needed a summer job. Where would I be without the sound advice of my resourceful cousin Rudy? He told me that Atlantic City, New Jersey, had plenty of waitressing opportunities for college students. So right after school let out, I packed my bags and headed for Atlantic City, traveling, once again, on a Greyhound bus. Even though I had never been a waitress, I was confident that I would find a job quickly. After all, how much skill does it take to carry food on a tray? I would find out.

I was expecting Atlantic City to be a tony resort town, much like Westhampton Beach, but it was a dump. Many of the buildings were dilapidated multifamily dwellings, the streets were dirty, and there were shady-looking people milling around the bus station. Wasting no time, I put my bags in a locker and began to walk the streets looking for room-for-rent signs.

I was used to my little adventures of finding a place to live, but this time I was really out of my comfort zone. It was getting dark, and I didn't know a soul. I must have looked scared and nervous, because when I knocked on the door of a house that had a room-for-rent sign, the woman took one look at me and, even though the room had been rented, she offered to let me stay in a spare bedroom for at least that night. Thank God! I was afraid that I would have had to spend the night at the bus station with a bunch of strangers. I'm sure that God sent this woman as my guardian angel. The expression "God looks out for babies and fools" applied to me in this situation. The very next day I found a room at a boardinghouse.

Now that I had a place to live, I was ready to search for a waitressing job. After a few unsuccessful attempts, I came to the Seaside Hotel, an upscale hotel right on the boardwalk. I was approached by an elderly black man who asked whether I needed help. I will always remember Harvey with great fondness. When I told him that I was there to apply for a job as a waitress, he, of course, asked what you would expect any hiring manager to ask: "Have you ever been a waitress before?"

Having learned from my Macy's experience, I answered in the affirmative. Smiling broadly at me, he handed me a large, oval-shaped, aluminum tray and asked me to walk across the room carrying the tray. This seemed like an easy enough request, so with the grace of a ballerina, I waltzed across the room carrying the tray on my fingertips. He gave me an inscrutable look, but without another word, he said, "You're hired." I congratulated myself, thinking that I obviously had a natural talent for waitressing.

That summer I gained new insight into how the pecking order played out between the veteran waitstaff and the patrons of the elegant Seaside Hotel, a resort that catered to well-heeled families who returned year after year. For a few weeks, if not the entire summer, vacationers entered the stately, chandelier-lit dining room. The waitstaff nodded politely and took its cue as the head of a family requested a specific table and a specific server from previous years.

This was a good arrangement for employees who were there for years and who had established a good working relationship with the families. They cornered the market, so to speak, and got the best families who left the best tips. As any person who waits on tables knows, the money is in the tips. As the new kid on the block, I was outranked and ordered to wait on either first-time vacationers and/or lousy tippers. Harvey came to my rescue, however, and intervened on my behalf, making sure that I got my share of good tippers.

On the final day of employment at the end of the summer, Harvey asked me to come see him before I left. Our conversation started with the usual pleasantries. He asked me how my summer had gone, to which I responded, "Very well." Then out of the blue, he hit me with a zinger: "Lillian, now tell me the truth.

Had you ever waited on tables before this summer?" Knowing that I had been found out, I looked at him sheepishly and responded, "No." He replied, "I knew you hadn't." With a puzzled look on my face, I asked, "How did you know?" He replied, "An experienced waitress knows that you do not carry a heavy tray of food on the tips of your fingers. Instead, you carry it in the palm of your hand. Your fingers are not strong enough to hold the tray." I was shocked and ashamed. "Then why did you hire me?" I asked. He replied, "You seemed so determined that I decided to give you a chance." That day, this wise and remarkable man became another guardian angel who helped me along my way.

*   *   *

In the fall of 1963 I was back in D.C. for my second year at Howard. Having made a decision not to return to the dorm, I pored over the room-for-rent ads—it was beginning to feel like the story of my life—and spotted what I hoped would be an affordable room in a neighborhood of row houses close to campus. My hopes were dashed when the landlady took me down a flight of stairs to the basement into a small, dark, dingy room.

Another young woman had apparently seen the same ad in the newspaper and was looking at the same room. As our paths crossed, we made eye contact and in that instant became "partners in crime." This newly found acquaintance, Geraldine, became my roommate and then my friend for the rest of my undergraduate years. Since it was late in the day and there were twin beds in the room, we decided to team up and take the room with the intention of finding another place—the sooner the better. Not a day went by that we didn't have our noses stuck in the newspaper, scouring the want ads for better living accommodations.

That's how we found our dear landlady, Mrs. Azalein Hawkins. We knew that we had struck gold the minute we arrived on Oak Street NW, a well-maintained black neighborhood of tidy row houses conveniently located near campus. Better yet, it was near a bus stop, which was a real advantage for two college students who had to shuttle back and forth to school. The landlady greeted us warmly, showing us a well-lit, cheerful room with twin beds on the second floor. It was a perfect arrangement, especially because this kind, middle-aged woman seemed genuinely interested in our welfare, peppering us with questions about school and what we were studying.

Quick to share information about herself, Mrs. Hawkins told us about the people who lived with her—her thirteen-year-old daughter and an older sister—and her large Doberman pinscher. She also told us that she had a son who was away at college. From the minute we agreed to be boarders, Mrs. Hawkins took us into her circle of friends and relatives and treated us as if we were her own children. This gave me a warm feeling, similar to when I lived with the Trents, and I began to realize just how deep, steadfast, and unconditional the bond between black people can be in our efforts to help one another find our place in the sun. Like Marie Trent, Mrs. Hawkins invited me to join her church, which I gladly did. (Marie Trent and Azalein Hawkins were cut from the same cloth, and I saw them both as my adopted mothers.)

Mrs. Hawkins turned out to be a peach in other ways. Understanding the plight of struggling and hungry students, she habitually came to the foot of the stairs and called to us to come down for dinner. Homemade dinners had not been part of our agreement, but she was one of the most generous people I have ever met. In fact, on the day of my graduation, you would have thought it was her own child who was graduating. She always welcomed my mother to stay with us when my mother visited me at school, but when it was time for me to graduate, Mrs. Hawkins invited my entire family—my parents, siblings, and many other relatives—to stay with her while they attended the graduation ceremony. Her gesture taught me something about the strength of the black network: we rejoice in the achievements of one another because an individual achievement is really the collective achievement of our race.

The biggest and saddest event of my sophomore year was the assassination of President Kennedy. What had begun to be a positive time in the United States with his election turned dark and frightening in less than three years. The day President Kennedy was assassinated felt like the end of the world. From the news coverage on the morning of November 22, 1963, there was no indication that our president would be in any kind of danger as his motorcade drove through the streets of Dallas. I imagined it to be a festive day, with parades and people cheering and waving as this handsome, idealistic man smiled and waved to his adoring fans.

I was in class when a voice came over the loudspeaker announcing that President Kennedy had just been shot. Although the school administration tried to keep things under control, the campus could not be contained. People were screaming, crying, hugging, and praying. By the time I left my class to run across campus to Founders Library, where I was scheduled to work, the voice over the loudspeaker announced, "The president of the United States, John F. Kennedy, is dead." The news ripped through the campus like wildfire. By the time I got to the library, I learned that the university, including the library, had been shut down. Catching the bus home, I was overcome with an inconsolable sadness.

On that day, the black community mourned as if we had lost a personal friend. We had come to see President Kennedy as our beacon of hope as an advocate for civil rights. The collective mind of black people was besieged with questions: Where is our country headed? What's going to happen to our civil rights? What's going to become of the black race? The hope, the promise, and the progress all seemed to vanish that day.

*　　*　　*

My studies were more varied and relevant in my sophomore year, but I still wasn't sure about declaring a major. I had a fleeting thought of majoring in fashion design because I loved clothes and the feel of luxurious fabrics, but I wasn't ready to commit.

Besides, one of the courses, "Introduction to Business," was beginning to pique my interest. The course was taught by Professor H. Naylor Fitzhugh, and there was something about this professor that impressed me.

Never in my life had I heard a black person speak with such conviction and eloquence about business and our race. I was transfixed by his words, "Business is a way for blacks to take control of their destiny." I had a great deal to learn about the world of business, and I began to think about my future in relation to what these words meant. His classroom instruction was something else. Instead of delivering the usual boring, rote lectures, Professor Fitzhugh used a teaching technique called the *case method,* which, I would later learn, was the signature method used at none other than Harvard Business School, from which Professor Fitzhugh had graduated in 1933. The case method challenged students to analyze a business problem or situation and formulate a decision based on their own analysis.

Professor Fitzhugh developed and presented a description of a business situation, which was no more than two pages, and left his students with a cliffhanger question: "What would you do?" I was fascinated by this way of thinking: there were no right or wrong answers, but the quality of your decisions was based on your ability to understand the underlying issues of the problem and to think things through in an orderly and logical fashion. I understood intuitively that this was exactly how people made decisions in real life, which made this method even more relevant to me.

What more could a human being ask for? I was being given the opportunity to sharpen my analytical and problem-solving skills to make better decisions. This was education at its best. I began to think that I was hardwired for a career in business, so when I talked to Professor Fitzhugh about majoring in business, he was more than encouraging. He suggested that I concentrate in marketing, which was his area of expertise. Since I had such respect for him and looked up to him as a mentor, I followed his advice.

My relationship with Professor Fitzhugh became life altering the day he hired me to be his student assistant and typist for his doctoral dissertation. It was an honor when a professor asked a student, who had to be in good academic standing, to be his or her assistant. I gladly performed my administrative duties, such as typing exams and syllabi, answering the phone, making appointments, and proctoring exams.

I can't explain why Professor Fitzhugh took a personal interest in me. Perhaps it was because his mother, of whom he spoke affectionately, and I had the same first name. Or perhaps he saw me as a fish out of water—an older student struggling to fit in yet determined to create her own destiny. For whatever reason, he took me under his wing and began slowly but surely turning me in a new direction.

Professor Fitzhugh was funny without trying to be, and I found his earnest gestures to be endearing. For example, he'd rush into the classroom—he was always in a hurry—carrying an armful of books. He greeted the class with a crisp, formal "Good afternoon." Without wasting another moment or gesture, he would proceed to take roll call every day until he learned all his students' names. After that, he'd simply look at each student individually and check off his or her name in his little black book. For the first few days, as he was just getting to know his students, I'd see him make some kind of notation as he called roll. I imagined that this was his way of noting specific characteristics about each of his students in order to correlate the name to the face. Once he got to know our names, he would always address us formally, as Mr., Mrs., or Miss So-and-So.

There was also a humorous side to Professor Fitzhugh that would sneak up on you and catch you off guard. For example, there was a protocol for posting grades. At the beginning of the semester, a professor would assign students random ID numbers. Final grades were posted outside the classroom next to your assigned number. How well I remember the day that Professor Fitzhugh handed out the assigned numbers for his Introduction to Business class. My number was accompanied by a handwritten note that said, "Someone had to get it." I looked incredulously at the number "13." What was he telling me? What does this mean? I tried to make light of it, telling myself that I wasn't at all superstitious. At the end of the semester, number 13 got an A in his course. Since that day, I have considered 13 to be my lucky number.

Professor Fitzhugh's unassuming disposition belied an extraordinary man who was a giant among mortals. Just shy of six feet tall, he was a stocky man with medium brown skin who wore heavy rimmed glasses, but usually just for reading. His partly gray hair and a receding hairline made him look distinguished. He always wore a suit—as did most of the other professors— but behind his formal facade, if you looked very closely at him, there was something about his mischievous smile that gave you a glimpse into the depth of this man.

H. Naylor Fitzhugh was born in Washington, D.C., in 1909 and received an academic scholarship to Harvard College at the age of sixteen. When he graduated with honors in 1931, he was one of only four blacks in a class of about a thousand students. I came across an interview that he had given to Harvard Business School's student newspaper, *The HarBus,* in which he spoke about this experience:

> I was fortunate to have grown up in a very stable and happy situation at home, in school, and at church. In addition, I had received so much encouragement at Dunbar [an all-black high school in Washington, D.C., renowned for academic excellence] that I felt confident about my ability to continue my studies successfully at Harvard. The rest of the "Harvard experience" was completely outside my ken. For example, although Harvard in the 1920s provided blacks with equal opportunities for an education, it didn't allow us to live in the dormitories with the other students. Instead, we lived with black families in Cambridge.

His story doesn't end there. After graduating from Harvard College, he went across the Charles River to Harvard Business

School, where he was one of the first blacks to attend and the only black person in his class. Graduating in 1933, he was one of the first blacks to receive a Harvard MBA. Upon graduation, however, no company recruited him, so he returned to Washington, D.C., and became an independent salesman, working part time for several printing firms within the black community, selling business cards, wedding invitations, and restaurant menus.

In the aforementioned newspaper article, Professor Fitzhugh goes on to describe the double injustice of being a well-educated black man of his time: "At Harvard I was never approached by a recruiter. Indeed, even if I'd wanted it, I couldn't have obtained a job as a grocery clerk in a chain store unit in an all-black neighborhood in Washington." During the early days of segregation, chain stores were owned by whites, and a clerk job was considered to be too good a job to be given to a black person, even if the black person would be working in a black community.

Naylor Fitzhugh was more than a salesman; he became a leader in the black community when he created the New Negro Alliance of Washington. This organization led protests and ultimately pursued landmark legal action against major companies that did business in black neighborhoods but refused to hire black employees. His prominent position brought him to the attention of some Howard University administrators, who asked him if he would teach a business course at the university. Having previously eliminated teaching as a career option, he nevertheless agreed to accept the position, because it was supposed to be for just one semester. That was 1934. As fate would have it, he was bitten by the teaching bug, and he stayed on as a full-time faculty member for the next three decades, taking time out for two years to pursue graduate work at Columbia University and American University.

Earning the epithet "Dean of Black Business," Naylor Fitzhugh's legacy at Howard became legendary. Over the next thirty years, he had only one objective—to change the landscape for blacks in the field of business. His involvement in organizing Howard

University's Small Business Development Center and chairing its advisory committee is evidence of his commitment to improve the business environment for black students. Small business development centers were created to provide management assistance to small business owners through easily accessible branch locations throughout the country. The centers are typically located on college campuses and are a cooperative effort of the private sector, the educational community, and federal, state, and local governments.

How fortunate, then, that I became one of Professor Fitzhugh's beneficiaries and later a devotee. I took most of my business courses from him and made marketing my major largely because he taught those courses. I came to appreciate the shrewdness in his approach to me. Just as in his teaching of the case method, he let me think that I was making my own decisions. For example, he explained to me the importance of being a well-rounded student and that being involved in extracurricular activities would strengthen my résumé when I started interviewing with prospective employers. Thus, I became actively involved in the Business and Marketing clubs and became president of both.

I got to know another side of Professor Fitzhugh in the Business Club. His commitment to his students ran deep. He arranged annual field trips to major corporations to expose us to different types of businesses. The trip I remember most was to Detroit, Michigan, when we traveled by bus to visit the General Motors facility. He handled every detail of the trip to ensure that we got the most out of the experience. From the moment we arrived, we were greeted and treated respectfully as young and promising businessmen and businesswomen. We met with senior staff, of whom we could ask questions, and we received a deluxe tour of the plant. We were also well fed.

Taking to heart Professor Fitzhugh's advice about being well-rounded, I also decided to pledge a sorority. I chose Zeta Phi Beta because it was one of the smaller sororities, and I have always preferred small groups. I had not completely overcome my shyness.

Zeta Phi Beta sorority also had the reputation of taking their academics more seriously than some of the other sororities did. I was especially pleased with my choice when I discovered that Professor Fitzhugh's mother had been a Zeta.

*   *   *

My junior year at Howard was a turning point. I had not seriously considered graduate school until Professor Fitzhugh began talking to me about it. I should have known by now that this professor, with his cunning smile, was light-years ahead of me. One day he suddenly turned to me and asked, "Are you going to graduate school?" I don't know why I responded the way I did, for I had no intention of continuing my education, but I blurted out, "I'm thinking about it." The way he asked the question suggested that he naturally assumed that I would be going, and I didn't want to disappoint him.

His question started me thinking, though. I had so much respect for this man that I began to think that if he thought I should go to graduate school, then perhaps I should consider it. Knowing that this question would come up again, I thought it best to have some names of graduate schools in mind so I could rattle off a few that sounded impressive. A short time later, he asked me what graduate schools I was considering. I responded with a well-stocked list of names: University of Michigan, University of Chicago, and Stanford University.

Raising an eyebrow, he asked, "Why not Harvard?" My jaw dropped. Going to Harvard was not something I could ever imagine. My perception of Harvard students was that they were rich blue bloods and geniuses as well. Professor Fitzhugh was about to change that perception by instilling in me that I was "Harvard material" and that I had every right to go to Harvard Business School.

Professor Fitzhugh wasn't the only one who had this thought. I am sure there was a conspiracy. Dr. Wilford White, the director of the Small Business Development Center, joined forces with

Professor Fitzhugh to convince me to apply to Harvard Business School. Dr. White, a white man who had received his doctorate from Harvard, turned out to be a champion of black students and black business owners. Since becoming director of the center, he had helped to expand the center's influence by bringing black business students and black business owners together on projects that would be mutually beneficial. Students would get credit for helping to solve business owners' problems.

In retrospect, I'm amused by the vastly different approaches these two professors used to convince me that applying to Harvard was the only thing for a smart, ambitious young woman to do. Professor Fitzhugh used the Socratic method of persuasion, asking probing, indirect questions and allowing me to arrive at my own decision as if he had nothing to do with it. He simply presented the problem according to the case method. Professor White, however, was direct to the point of being blunt.

The saddest part of my otherwise exhilarating experience at Howard was the day Professor Fitzhugh told me that he had accepted an offer from Pepsi-Cola and that he would not be returning to Howard in the fall, which would be my senior year. This was a crushing blow: I was losing my mentor and part of my soul. I would soon learn that he had declined several offers from major corporations over the years, but this time he received an offer that he couldn't refuse. Pepsi had recruited him to be vice president of special markets. He was following in the footsteps of a line of prominent black executives who were recruited by Pepsi, beginning in 1940 with the hiring of a single black sales-man, Herman T. Smith.

This was a remarkable, if not revolutionary, move for a public company of its day, but as explained in Stephanie Capparell's book, *The Real Pepsi Challenge,* Pepsi recognized the untapped power of the black consumer in its efforts to unseat its number one rival, Coca-Cola. Professor Fitzhugh was lured to Pepsi by Harvey C. Russell, a rising black Pepsi executive who had just been promoted to vice president of corporate planning of the newly formed PepsiCo, Inc. (created through the merger of Pepsi-Cola and Frito-Lay).

As vice president of special markets, Naylor Fitzhugh would come to be known as the creator of target marketing in corporate America by identifying the African American consumer as a lucrative and distinct market.

Thus, my junior year ended on a melancholy note. I would no longer have Professor Fitzhugh as a teacher, nor would I be his assistant. Nevertheless, in his inimitable, charitable, graceful style, he made sure that I would have a teacher's assistant job in my senior year. He introduced me to his replacement, Professor Thomas Douglas, a white man in his late fifties, and recommended that he retain me as his student assistant. On the last day that I worked for Professor Fitzhugh, we exchanged pleasant but sad good-byes, with the promise that we would stay in touch. We honored that promise. On his visits to Washington, D.C., to attend high school class luncheons at his alma mater, Dunbar, we sometimes met for lunch or dinner. I even attended some of his Dunbar class luncheons.

Like most college seniors, I existed in two diametrically opposed worlds: the predictable world of today and the unknown world of tomorrow. For what seemed like a fleeting moment, I gave myself permission to enjoy my final days at Howard before I had to think about more pressing demands, like applying to graduate school or, more to the point, applying to Harvard Business School.

Although I wasn't totally convinced that I really wanted to continue my academic studies, I hadn't given much thought to what else I would do. Besides, I didn't think I had much of a choice. I was caught between two formidable forces, Professor Fitzhugh and Dr. White, and the die was cast. Even though Naylor Fitzhugh was now at Pepsi, I could feel his influence bearing down on me as he whispered in my ear, *Lillian, you're Harvard material. You can do it.* Dr. White's influence was more tangible: direct: he simply handed me a Harvard Business School application with specific instructions to apply now.

Dr. White proceeded to review my application and showed me how to strengthen my essays, which he said were the most important part of the application. After I received his approval and blessings, I dropped the application in the mailbox while thinking, *What will be will be.* I was disappointed that I couldn't race back to Professor Fitzhugh's office to tell him of my accomplishment, but I did the next best thing: I imagined him giving me a pat on the back, assuring me that everything was going to work out fine.

*   *   *

Since graduate school was in my plans for the following fall (1966), I devoted my last semester at Howard to looking for a summer job. On one of my visits to the placement office, I noticed a posting for the NASA Spacecraft Center in Houston. I had never been to Houston, and I didn't even know anyone who lived there, but wanderlust was growing inside me, so I applied for the job and was accepted. All I could think of was, *I can add another city to my travel log.*

I couldn't wait to tell Mrs. Coombs of my good fortune. Initially, she seemed happy for me, but on a subsequent visit to her office she expressed concern when I told her that I hadn't given much thought as to where I would be living. This was all she needed to hear. The next time I saw her, she informed me that she had spoken to friends who lived in Houston and that they had agreed to let me stay with them for the summer. Mrs. Coombs had become another guardian angel who was there to protect and guide me.

Then something unexpected happened. Before heading off to Houston in early June 1966, I received notification that Harvard had rejected my application because my Graduate Management Admission Test (GMAT) scores weren't high enough. Although a rejection letter from Harvard would have devastated many, if not most, people, I wasn't crushed—disappointed, yes; devastated, no.

Having already overcome many challenges in my young adult life, I had begun to redefine the word *rejection*. To me it did not mean defeat; it just meant a temporary setback. I knew that I would find a way to turn this latest setback into a victory. I just needed time to come up with a strategy. An internal battle—my worthiness to go to Harvard, of which Professor Fitzhugh had convinced me—had already been won. Sticking to my original plan, I graduated cum laude from Howard and headed for Houston, where my summer job was waiting for me.

My new family and its cute white terrier welcomed me with open arms. The Smiths lived in a beautiful ranch-style house in an upscale black community. Mrs. Ernestine Smith was a homemaker, and Mr. Raymond Smith was a self-employed insurance agent. This was my first exposure to the way that upper-class black people lived, and it opened up a whole new world to me. I was impressed that the Smiths had a black housekeeper, a sweetheart of a lady, who cleaned and cooked for them. I recalled my days of working for the white family on Fifth Avenue and my desire to live as they did. Now, for the first time, I had met a black family who had a maid, so I quickly replaced the white family on Fifth Avenue in my mind's eye with a real-life black family to whom I could relate.

In time, I learned that Houston was a growing city with a strong black community in a section known as Third Ward, and my new family seemed to be the center of it. In fact, Mrs. Smith was a sophisticated socialite who frequently invited me to attend social affairs, receptions, cocktail parties, and formal dances. At the time, I thought it was merely a nice gesture that she invited me to such events, but it wasn't until I was out in the real world, making a name for myself in business, that I realized that Mrs. Smith gave me a first-class education on how to conduct myself when interacting with high society.

That summer, I decided how to handle my Harvard rejection. I wrote this venerable institution a letter expressing both disappointment and a strong desire to enroll in the MBA program.

The letter I received back was cordial but not entirely positive. I was simply told that I could reapply but that there were no guarantees of acceptance. I was not the least bit discouraged. *No guarantees are needed,* I thought. I would get in. I began studying for the GMAT, determined to improve my score and keep my sights on Harvard.

With graduate school now on hold, I had to find another job as the NASA job was just a summer internship. Since D.C. was a place that I knew well and had grown to love, I made a decision to move back and find a job there. That's when I heard about a position as secretary to the deputy managing editor at the *Washington Post*. I got the job, and at age twenty-six, I returned to D.C. and found my first apartment, a studio, which was a short distance from where I had lived while I was at Howard. I liked the *Post,* and I especially enjoyed learning how the news developed behind the scenes. Most important, however, was that my job wasn't very taxing, which gave me the time I needed to study for and retake the GMAT exam.

After taking the GMAT in late 1966, I resubmitted my application to Harvard. In April, I received a letter of acceptance for the fall of 1967. Being admitted to Harvard was comparable to climbing to the top of Mt. Everest. Although I was initially lackadaisical about going to Harvard Business School, over time, I began to realize the significance of this institution. Considering all that I had to overcome to get myself to this point in my life, it finally sank in that this was a bigger deal than I was willing to admit. The only people I told that I was applying to Harvard were my parents, but when I received the good news that I'd been accepted, I wanted the whole world to know. Congratulations poured in from friends, relatives, and, of course, Professor Fitzhugh, who said that he would always be there for me.

Now that I knew that I would be going to Harvard Business School in the fall, I had to make a decision about my present circumstances. Although I enjoyed my time working at the *Post,*

I had come across a summer position in Houston with Humble Oil Company (now ExxonMobil). Learning that the pay would be better and that it was a higher-level position than my *Post* job, I applied and was hired. I contacted the Smiths, my adopted family in Houston, and they were delighted that I would be returning to spend the summer with them. As luck would have it, that summer I met Roy Lincoln, the man who would become my husband.

5

Harvard Business School: 1967–1968

I was in Harvard, but not of it.

—W. E. B. DuBois, Harvard University's first black Ph.D. (class of 1895)

I arrived in Boston after a ten-hour train ride from Washington, D.C. The train was all I could afford; flying was simply too expensive. With one large oversized trunk—the kind that college students used back then—and a suitcase in my hand, I hailed a cab. My destination was Cambridge. I'd been up North before, but everything about New England felt different, including the crisp, brisk air. New Englanders, I imagined, must be the same.

The cab driver dropped me off on Ash Street in front of my dorm, which was a large, nondescript brick building. I knocked on the door and was greeted by a stern, matronly woman in her fifties. She looked every bit the dorm mother. With barely a glance, she asked me my last name, strolled nonchalantly over to a desk, and casually checked off *Hobson* on her list. In a clipped tone, she told me that my room wouldn't be ready until 3 p.m. It was only 1 p.m., and it appeared that I was the first student to arrive. Pointing to a park down the street—which I couldn't see from where I was standing—she suggested that I wait there until my room was ready. The friendliest part of the exchange was when she told me that I could leave my bags in the foyer. Welcome to Harvard!

I headed toward the park in a trance. After my long trip, the bench looked inviting, at least more inviting than the dorm mother. I sat down wearily. At that moment it sank in that I was actually at Harvard, arguably the most prestigious university in the country and one of the most famous universities in the world. I was suddenly overcome with fear, the kind that turns you upside down inside. Alone in a strange place, I was about to embark on a journey that would take me far away from anything I had ever known or could relate to. I thought, *How did I, a poor black farm girl from Ballsville, Virginia, end up here?*

In utter despair, I shook my head and cried out, "Why am I here?" In that instant, I wanted nothing more than to board the next train home. I was twenty-seven years old and homesick in a way I'd never been for my family, relatives, and friends. Self-doubt was creeping into my being, and I began to question whether coming to Harvard was the right thing to do.

I was clearly at the breaking point when I took control of my emotions and told myself to get a grip. Suddenly the faces of all the people who believed in me and who had played a huge part in helping me to get here flashed before my eyes.

There was my dear mother, the former schoolteacher who wanted nothing more than for her daughter to continue her education, and Professor Fitzhugh, my mentor at Howard University. There was Dr. White, the other professor at Howard who had handed me a Harvard Business School (HBS) application and commanded that I apply. There was my cousin Rudy, who kept nagging me to stop wasting my time in menial jobs and go to college. Last but not least, there was my father, who didn't even know the name of the school I would be attending but was so proud to tell everyone that "Lillian is going to the same school that President Kennedy went to." Reflecting on all these people, I knew the course of my life was set: I had a responsibility, and I could not disappoint the people who supported me. There was no looking back and there was no turning away; I had to move forward.

With new resolve, I walked back to the dorm. The reeducation of Lillian Hobson was about to begin. My first big surprise—and believe me, there would be many more—was learning that my dorm wasn't on the Harvard Business School campus but was located half a mile away across the Charles River. No one had told me that female MBA students weren't allowed to live on the business school campus. (This all changed by 1971 when the campus became fully coed and female MBA students were allowed to live on campus.)

I hadn't had the means, nor did I even think it was necessary, to visit the school before I accepted its offer: When Harvard accepts you, you go. In time, I would learn that women weren't admitted to the MBA program until 1963. That year, eight pioneering women were the first to graduate with an MBA degree. Before 1963, the school awarded women a certificate in business administration.

According to a Harvard Business School Centennial retrospective article on the history of women at HBS, business training for women from 1937 to 1962 was seen as "the first daring experiment in practical education." When I arrived in 1967, only eighteen women, including me, out of eight hundred students were enrolled in the first-year MBA program. Had I known beforehand much of what I would learn in the next two years about the B-School, as Harvard Business School is commonly called, I don't think I would have had it in me to go to Harvard.

Nothing on this good earth could have prepared me for Harvard Business School—the ultimate "ivory tower" sitting mightily above the treetops, untouched by the war protests and the racial unrest that were rocking the rest of the country at the time. If small things inform larger issues, this was the case with the geographic location of HBS in Boston in relation to Harvard University's main campus in Cambridge, across the Charles River. Apparently, not only did the river separate the B-School's female MBAs from its male MBAs, but the Charles—as New Englanders call it—symbolized the Great Divide, separating Harvard's liberals from its conservative counterparts.

In those days, Harvard University students on the main campus often referred to the Harvard Business School campus as "the West Point of American capitalism" and its students as "capitalist pigs." The clash between the two types of students was stunning. I can only imagine the snide remarks that were hurled across the river as the business students rushed to class: "Who are these freaks in gray flannel suits?" "What kind of a profession is business, anyway? You aren't studying to be a lawyer or a doctor? So what *are* you studying to be?" HBS students were thick-skinned, however, or so it seemed, and nothing could break their stride. They didn't seem to care that they were out of step with the rest of Harvard University or, for that matter, with the rest of the country.

If male MBA students in their gray flannel suits stuck out like sore thumbs in this liberal part of the country during the late 1960s, it must have been even more freakish to see a handful of female students at Harvard Business School. I'm sure we looked ridiculous to the rest of the world as we dashed across the bridge from Cambridge, braving the bitter cold and wind to get to class.

Like our male counterparts, we were impeccably dressed in our corporate best, which for women meant business suits, nylon stockings, and high heels. The irony here is that although female MBA students were considered to be out of step with the times, my generation of women who were pursuing MBA degrees was in the vanguard: we were trailblazers, preparing ourselves to be professional businesswomen who would compete in a man's world.

*   *   *

I must have been dead tired by the time I laid my head on the pillow that first night because I don't recall a single event or a single face from that day. All I know is that the next morning I found myself in the dorm foyer with a group of women, and we were about to take our maiden voyage across the river to register for class. I put on the cheerful face of a schoolgirl setting out on her first day of school. With a mixture of excitement and nervousness, I was determined to see it as another adventure.

When we arrived at Baker Library, I was in awe of the number of students who were coming and going in an efficient, competent, self-absorbed manner. I later learned that there were 1,387 students—first- and second-year students combined—registering for class that day. I picked up my registration packet and examined the contents: my class schedule, the names of my professors, and a personalized white cardboard nameplate (eighteen inches long and four inches high) with my name spelled out in large black letters. I studied my nameplate. Never in my life had I seen my name in such large print: LILLIAN HOBSON. It was official. I had arrived at Harvard.

By the end of the day, my excitement had all but dissolved. The antiseptic, white-glove world of this institution had begun to reveal itself in strange but telling ways. For starters, I had learned that first-year students were assigned to a specific class section (ranging from A to H), with approximately a hundred students in each section. I was assigned to Section D, which, in typical B-School parlance, would be my "lifetime section." In other words, my assigned section would be the way in which the school would identify me for the rest of my life—and I do mean for the rest of my life. Every form of communication that I would ever receive from the school would bear the Section D label.

In time, I would also learn that the nameplates were a professor's secret "cold call" weapon: students could not hide from or escape the gaze of an omnipotent professor, who at a moment's notice could glance at your nameplate, address you as Miss or Mr. So-and-So, and ask you to explain a complicated business situation.

I'll never forget the fateful day that I got my first cold call. You could hear a pin drop as the professor waited for me to expound intelligently on a case study. Although I tried to collect myself and speak up, I froze and could only blurt out, "I have not read the case." There would be other days on which I would be prepared for a cold call, but unfortunately, this was not one of them. Some nights the workload was so heavy that I had to decide whether to read a case thoroughly or skim it just enough to get by. Until now I'd gotten away with skimming. Now came his admonition: "So, Miss Hobson, you are not prepared!" At that moment I just wanted to disappear into the woodwork. This was mockery and public humiliation, Harvard style.

My real descent into this strange new world came at the orientation for first-year students. I could hardly believe my eyes as I approached the stadium, which to me looked just like the Roman Colosseum; only the lions were missing. Apparently this venue was the only place large enough to hold eight hundred students. After I found a seat in the open arena, I turned to look at my classmates.

It was only then that I came to the realization of my circumstances. I thought, *This can't be*, as I began to count the dark faces in the stadium. *One, two, there's a third, there's a fourth.* The total number of blacks, excluding myself, came to only five. I couldn't believe it. *There must be more of us*, I desperately thought. I counted the faces again and got the shock of my life: *There are six dark faces in this place, and oh my Lord, I'm the only black woman!*

I was used to being a minority in plenty of other situations, but I was shaken to my core to learn that I was the only black woman in the first-year class at Harvard Business School. It was probably bad enough to be a white woman, because there were only seventeen of them in 1967, but to be a black woman was revolutionary, as I would eventually find out. It was only after I graduated from Harvard Business School that I was told that I had made history as the first black woman to receive a Harvard MBA.

This was not the time to dwell on my unique situation, however, because before I knew it a large-framed, burly-looking man took the stage. Dean George P. Baker was at least six feet tall and had a pronounced air of sophistication and authority. I don't recall much of what he said, except for this one piece of advice: "Take full advantage of the case method [of teaching] because it may be the only time in your life when you can make a decision and not have to live with it." I didn't fully understand what he meant until

I was out in the business world, when, in fact, I did have to live with my decisions, for better or worse.

*   *   *

After my unnerving discoveries on registration day, I braced myself for the first day of class. Section D had ninety-seven white men and two other women besides me. I sat behind my nameplate in the third row of an elevated horseshoe-shaped classroom, feeling forlorn and self-conscious. My thoughts flashed back to Howard and how comfortable I had felt in a classroom where my race was the majority. Now I was just thankful for having an assigned seat between two kind, gregarious classmates who smiled at me and made small talk. I tried smiling back, but it was hard trying to keep up appearances. I think they understood my tenuousness.

It didn't take long for me to understand the gravity of my circumstances: no one at Harvard, including the faculty and the administrators, really knew what to make of me or what to do with me. I was the sole black woman in the whole place—there wasn't a single black female administrator, much less a black female professor. It's human nature for people who are uncomfortable with people whom they don't know how to approach to respond in the least confrontational manner: they ignore them. That's how the faculty and the administrators responded to me. They ignored me.

For example, on occasion, when I'd pass a professor in the hall, I could hear his footsteps quicken as he approached me. With barely an audible grunt, a forced smile, and downcast eyes, he'd rush past me as if he were running down a ramp to catch the next flight out of town. Perhaps my expectations were too high to think that a B-School professor would have the wherewithal or interest to stop and talk to this black woman, just to see how she was doing. A simple courtesy—"How are you doing?"—would have sufficed.

I was not the only one who was having a hard time, however. Many of my female classmates also felt the strain of being a minority. Some of us could have made the case that there was a pact between the all-male faculty and the male students. The professors were inclined to call on the men—the outspoken ones, that is—to lead classroom discussions. Their reason for doing this was most likely to ensure that classroom participation would be provocative, substantive, and even entertaining, as the nature of the case method demanded.

A little background on the case method, the B-School's trademark, will shed light on the demands that were placed on the students to perform in the classroom. Pioneered by HBS faculty in the 1920s, the case method describes a real-life business situation or problem. Students are asked to analyze and formulate an appropriate strategy and action based on the information presented. A case averages about fifty pages or more and containes sophisticated financial data, countless charts, and bell-curve graphs. It's bad enough to have to digest and analyze reams of information for one case study, but when a typical night's workload included two or three case studies, you can appreciate how grueling it was to prepare for classes the next day.

Since most of the male students were older (the average age was twenty-eight) and had real-world corporate experience, they were thought to be better equipped to assimilate and analyze the case studies. Although I had been exposed to the case method when I studied with Professor Fitzhugh at Howard, the cases he prepared were much shorter and simpler. Professor Fitzhugh's intention was to give us a taste of this method of problem solving. In addition, he made up his own cases, whereas the B-School's cases were prepared by professional teams who spent a great deal of time researching actual companies and culling financial reports and problematic situations.

With the exception of me and perhaps a few others, the women were younger and had come directly from undergraduate school. Since they had no real practical work experience, many of them (including me) were reluctant to speak up in class for fear of sounding, God forbid, *stupid*! Never before had I been in such a testosterone-fueled classroom, with some of the most aggressive men on earth. Their hands shot up in the air like rockets as soon as a professor posed a question, and they started shouting out the answer like falling bombs—what I called "fighting for air time"—while most of the women remained stone silent.

The contrast between the men and the women was stark. One of my classmates, Nancy Schenk, put it this way many years later: "I refused to talk at all. As a matter of principle, I wasn't going to talk in class. I didn't care about my grades. I figured as long as I got out, I was doing just fine." As a result, many of the female students suffered because a large part of the final grade was based on class participation.

Robin Foote was an exception among the mostly silent women, but it came with a price, as she recently confessed in a phone conversation: "I didn't shy away from class participation. I did what the guys did. I raised my hand, asked questions, and made comments. For me, the way to learn is to engage, which was against the norm [for the women]. I guess I was violating an established, unwritten social norm, [because] there were a lot of people—the men—who were p—ed off at me and probably hated my guts." Being true to herself, Robin made history as the first woman to graduate at the top of the class as a Baker Scholar.

* * *

The immensity of the academic challenges that beset the female sex became clear to me one night when I was sitting in my small, bare dorm room, which was furnished with a single bed, a clothes closet, and a desk piled high with papers. There I was with my prized possession, my radio, which gave me what little pleasure and diversion I could squeeze out of this pressure-cooker environment.

That particular night I was listening to songs by my favorite artists—the Temptations, Gladys Knight and the Pips, the Four

Tops, and the Platters—as I stared at all the work that lay before me: long, boring, grueling case studies. I wondered how the other women in the dorm were tackling their studies. In one of our orientations, we were told that study groups offered the best method for dealing with the heavy course load. It was also highly recommended that students form study groups with people from their own section, not with students from another section.

One of the main problems with the study-group arrangement was that most of them met in the evening on the business school campus. This posed a problem for the women living in the Radcliffe dorm; none of us wanted to walk across the river in the dark, and there was no such thing as a shuttle bus. In my case, I hadn't been invited to join a group, nor did I have a clue as to how the selection process worked. After considering my options, I gave up the idea altogether, which meant that I would have to make it through Harvard on my own, without the benefit and support of a study group.

However, I wasn't alone in choosing not to be part of a study group. Although Carolyn Keller and Robin Foote joined a study group, they were the exception. Why it never occurred to the rest of us women to start our own group in the Radcliffe dorm is beyond me. If we had done so, we would have had to form a group made up of students from different sections—a configuration that was not recommended. In hindsight, a study group of our own making—regardless of the rules—would have been better than none at all.

As a result, women were put at another serious disadvantage in the classroom, which we all learned the hard way. The beauty of a study group was that it made the course load more manageable because the cases were divvied among the study group's members. Each person was responsible for mastering his or her assigned case and then discussing it with the group. When the class met, every student in the study group was prepared to discuss all of the cases.

In effect, a study group was a student's lifeline and survival kit. Many years later, the school introduced learning teams and made them mandatory. Today, all first-year students are assigned to a learning team, and during the year each team is assigned projects that require its members to work together. While study groups are still optional, they are in addition to learning teams.

After a few months, I mustered up the nerve to approach one of my professors and explain to him that I was finding it virtually impossible to keep up with three cases a night, every night. Having been humiliated once by the cold call, I refused to let it happen again, so I knew that I needed to take action to make sure that I was prepared for the next one, which was certain to come.

The professor looked at me quizzically. "You don't think we expect you to read all those cases every night, do you?" he asked. The look on my face must have expressed my shock and naiveté. It was beginning to sink in—finally—what this business school was all about. It was boot camp 101. We were being trained to be executives who would have to think on our feet, making decisions as they were thrown at us.

After that meeting, I made my own decision tree about how to tackle my studies based on the only kind of thinking I knew: practical, logical reasoning. Since it was impossible to study all three cases every night, I had to decide which of the three I would be (1) well prepared for, (2) somewhat prepared for, or (3) not at all prepared for. In making my decision, I considered the length and difficulty of the cases, which professor I thought would be the easiest on me if I were called on, and how much time I could realistically devote to studying on a particular night. This is how I chose to study from that point on, rationalizing to myself that this method was based on calculated risks rather than a guarantee of success.

*   *   *

Leave it to this prestigious school to create a universal, collective cold call that every first-year student was subjected to at the same time. It came in written form and was called a "written analysis of cases." Every HBS student can give you his or her version of the dreaded course, otherwise known as the WAC. Only Harvard Business School could come up with such a brain-hazing exercise, specifically designed to strike fear in the hearts of first-year students.

This is how it worked. Every six to eight weeks, the entire class was handed the same case on Friday afternoon (the last class of the week), which had to be turned in the following day, Saturday, by 5 p.m. on the dot. Need I tell you what most students were doing for twenty-four hours from Friday to Saturday? We must have looked quite a sight: a stream of crazed, blurry-eyed students tearing across campus, panting and gasping to get to Baker Library to drop our case analyses in a chute by 5:00 p.m., not 5:01.

As the campus bells tolled five, the chute slammed shut. A gathering of students had already formed to witness the race and see whether anyone had missed the deadline. As each person dropped his or her case into the black hole, the crowd let out a big roar, with the last person getting the loudest roar of all. God help the hapless person who missed the deadline.

To add insult to injury, the cases were then read and graded by "WAC readers," who were usually female graduates from Smith College or Wellesley College. To think that these women of privilege, with their fancy liberal arts degrees, were qualified to grade our knowledge of business was absurd. They may have known a thing or two about grammar and punctuation, which was evident from all the red marks strewn throughout the blue booklets, but they were hardly able to grade us on our analytical and problem-solving abilities.

The school dropped the WAC in 1993, after seventy-nine years of some version of this ritual. Some traditions at HBS die hard, however. So it was with this tradition, which remains in the annals of the school's institutional memory, as this quote from the September 2006 *Harvard Business School Bulletin* attests: "A plaque on the side of Baker Library memorializes the spot where students dropped their papers into a chute before it was shut tight at the final toll of the campus bell."

*   *   *

Because I lived on the Radcliffe campus, it seemed like an eternity before I finally got to meet my black classmates: Roy Willis, Clif Darden, Ted Lewis, George Price, and Carlson Austin. But it wasn't until I met Trish, Roy's wife, that I found a soft place to land. At last, here was a black woman to whom I could bare my soul. Trish was a godsend. The day we met we formed a lifelong friendship that has transcended HBS, marriages, and divorces. Roy and Trish lived off campus in a Harvard graduate student apartment in Peabody Terrace, and their home became my refuge on weekends.

Whereas I was perfectly content to bask in the warmth of the Willises' hospitality, Roy would not let creature comforts distract him from other things he deemed more important—in particular, bringing to the administration's attention his concern about the dearth of black students. Roy was incensed when he first arrived at HBS and walked into Section G only to find that he was the only black student in his section. Many years later, Roy recounted to me that he felt betrayed by Harvard, believing that this noble institution had misled him with false advertising. The Kennedy brothers (Jack and Bobby both went to Harvard) had been Roy's inspiration to come to HBS.

To Roy, it was bad enough to be a token black at his undergraduate alma mater, the University of Virginia—which he described as a racially hostile and isolating environment—but he had higher expectations of this northern institution, which was known for its liberal ideals. (Like many of us, Roy had assumed that the B-School espoused the same ideals as the rest of Harvard University.) Soon after Roy set foot on campus, he was on a mission, determined to shake the administration out of what he called its "sublime complacency."

Although the rest of us understood his angst, we were less inclined to take action. In fact, if Roy hadn't taken the lead, I don't think any of us would have had the courage to stand up to the business school and fight for our rights. Clif's view of his own situation at HBS is poignant:

> I came from academic environments in which I had always been "the only one" or, at best, "one of two or three." So initially I didn't think much about there being six black students. The situation seemed normal to me. Quite frankly, initially, my primary concern was doing well academically so that I could retain the Dwight D. Eisenhower Fellowship that made it possible for me to attend the B-School. I felt that I had a lot at stake. If I lost the scholarship, I would return home empty handed. Roy turned my thinking around when he made me see how thoroughly outrageous the situation was with the black population at HBS.

Clif became the first to follow Roy's lead, and together they became the ringleaders. Their first course of action was to make an appointment with the dean of students to voice their dissatisfaction. They thought the dean would be easy to approach because Clif knew him from his undergraduate days at the University of Southern California.

However, Clif and Roy were disappointed with the results of their initial meeting. Two opposing camps emerged: Roy and Clif focused on the paucity of black students, which the dean took as a personal criticism of his own efforts to increase the black student population. Apparently, when the dean of students came to the business school in 1966, he had taken personal responsibility for increasing the number of blacks from three to six in just a year. This was a 100 percent increase, which was not a bad statistic, as far as he was concerned.

Not only did he take offense at Clif and Roy's criticism of the school's progress in admitting black students, but he was also insulted because he thought he deserved some praise and recognition for his commitment to enrolling more black students. The meeting ended with bad feelings and an unresolved situation.

In fact, Clif claimed that this professor actually distanced himself from the black cause that very day. Despite this setback, Clif and Roy made a pact to take matters into their own hands until they secured a meeting with the higher-ups.

After many failed attempts, they were finally granted a meeting with some of the officers in the admissions department. Again they were rebuked. According to Roy, the administration dismissed them by saying, "You should be happy to be at Harvard. Don't waste your time on issues unrelated to your studies." The administration punctuated its reprimand by threatening to expel them if they persisted with their "aggression."

Roy, being who he was, responded in kind: "Do what you have to do, but we will not back down." The administration's seeming arrogance ignited both Roy and Clif. They hatched another plan and reached out to their black classmates, making a case for why we all should unite. It's amazing to see what can happen when you bring an entire population together for a cause (even if it is a population of just six).

I'll never forget how the tide turned one night in the early fall when Clif, Roy, and I gathered at Roy's home, as we frequently did. Sometime during the evening, our conversation turned to the underrepresentation of black students. This was the first time I had had a chance to open up and express my concerns about being the only black woman. It was then that I learned that Roy and Clif had already approached the administration a few times but had been rebuffed. As we talked through the evening, it became clear to the three of us that we had to do something for our own survival and for the survival of future generations of black students at the B-School.

That night we made up our own marching orders. The next day, Roy and Clif approached the other black students, Ted, Carlson, and George. Ted and George became involved immediately, but Carlson never joined the cause. By the end of the week, we had formed a team that turned out to be a good mix of talent, skills, and personalities.

Roy was our front man. Drawing on his experience at the University of Virginia, where he had been one of the first black students to integrate the university, he was fearless and invincible. It didn't hurt that he was the oldest among us and was a military veteran. We were impressed with his take-no-prisoners leadership style, and we felt bound to succeed with him as our leader.

Clif, the youngest member of the group, complemented Roy's aggressive approach. As the arch-strategist, he had the innate ability to prevent contested issues and conflicts from erupting into a donnybrook by encouraging us to calm down and focus on our objectives and our mission. Ted, George, and I worked as foot soldiers—a supportive role that would prove pivotal when the administration sought to dismiss Roy and Clif's demands as personal issues that were of no interest to the other black students in the class of 1969. Never underestimate what foot soldiers can do to further a cause; we could be counted on to show up for meetings with the administration. Our mere presence was proof that the situation was more than just a personal vendetta.

In the late fall of 1967, we scored a victory in a meeting with the legendary and imperious Dean Baker. Sitting behind his dark mahogany desk, he at first cut a larger-than-life image, but over the course of our meeting, his gruff facade softened considerably, to the point where he almost looked human that day. Roy, Clif, Ted, George, and I were in the meeting, but Roy did most of the talking. In his own inimitable style, he looked Dean Baker straight in the eye and asked him point-blank why the B-School had so few black students.

We were shocked by the dean's response: "We don't know where to find them." The chasm between Harvard and the black world could not have been more profound than at that moment. After all, this was the same institution that didn't seem to have a problem finding other minorities and foreign students.

The dean's statement took me back to when I was a senior at Howard and had met with a Harvard recruiter. It had struck me as odd that a place like Harvard thought it appropriate to send an older white man from Alabama with a strong southern accent to represent the business school. Now, sitting before an intelligent and powerful white man, I had my answer: white people like him were clueless about black people's visceral distrust of white southerners.

Dean Baker's admission of ignorance was all it took for us to define our mission. We declared to him right then and there that we would personally help HBS find and recruit qualified black students. He was impressed. How could he not be? We were willing to do a job that the business school was not equipped to do. The dean even offered to use his impressive corporate network to solicit financial aid for black candidates who couldn't afford the tuition. Shortly after the meeting, we met with the admissions office to develop a recruitment strategy.

* * *

By Thanksgiving, I was feeling a tremendous academic strain and was looking forward to going home and enjoying Mom's home cooking. My midterm grades were not very good, but I promised myself that they would improve. I was determined not to be a Thanksgiving dropout. Thanksgiving break was the point at which students who couldn't make the grade or who couldn't take the pressure did not return. I got a queasy feeling when I returned to campus after Thanksgiving and learned that one of the women in my section had dropped out. Now there was only one other woman besides me in Section D. Great—I would stick out even more.

Although I was pleased with myself for not becoming a dropout statistic, I was dogged by the advice that a Howard professor, who happened to be white, had once given to the mostly black population of Howard students: "If you go to both undergraduate and graduate schools, make sure one is a predominantly black institution and the other a predominantly white one." I was beginning to understand his advice. It meant that black people had to master the world of two very different cultures if they wanted to be successful in business and in life. At this stage, I knew I had to learn how to navigate the white world if I wanted to have a successful business career.

Even though I understood this advice on an intellectual level, it was a lot harder for me to put this wisdom into practice, because I had a hard time coming to terms with my feelings of loneliness and estrangement. Perhaps if I were more outgoing and less self-conscious, I could have forged friendships with my classmates, but after a few attempts at gaining membership to this exclusive club, I found socializing, especially attending HBS mixers, to be excruciatingly painful.

Can you imagine in those days a white boy coming up to a black girl and asking her to dance? Although interracial dating had been the subject of a hit song, *Society's Child* by Janis Ian, in 1966, and of a hit movie, *Guess Who's Coming to Dinner,* in 1967, Harvard was untouched by this emerging social phenomenon. What made matters worse is that my black male counterparts seldom attended the mixers because they had their own social circles: one was married, another was engaged, and at least one other lived off campus and had his own friends. As a result, I was never able to stretch my comfort zone to include mixing with my white classmates. Instead, I hung out with Trish as much as possible, and when that wasn't possible, I kept to myself. It was the best I could do.

Relief was on the way with the much-needed Christmas holiday. I could hardly contain my joy at getting away from my studies. Unfortunately, I disappointed my parents when I told them that I would not be coming home for Christmas. Instead, I would be visiting my boyfriend, Roy Lincoln. My parents knew nothing of my growing feelings for this man. They hadn't even met him.

I had met Roy the previous summer in Houston while I was working at Humble Oil. In fact, Roy tried to persuade me to stay in Houston and attend Rice University instead of "going North to that other institution," as he put it. I wouldn't think of it, however, especially after what I had gone through to be admitted to HBS.

As disappointed as my parents were that I was not coming home for Christmas, they had grown used to my surprises (and had even come to expect them), so they knew it was useless to convince their headstrong daughter to change her mind. Since finishing high school, I had always been away on some adventure. Mom once told me, "I'm not writing down your address in ink because you move too much. I'll keep it in pencil so I can erase it."

Roy and I had been writing to each other on a regular basis since I left for Harvard. Phone calls were few, because I didn't have a phone in my room and there was nothing worse than speaking to your beau on the public phone in the dorm hall. I loved receiving Roy's letters. He was a smooth talker, and his letters were always upbeat. His encouragement to "hang in there and get your degree" helped to keep me grounded as I struggled through my first semester. He also made me feel special in a way that no other man had up to that point in my life. I began to think he was the man with whom I could build a good life.

Our relationship had grown serious very quickly. Over the Christmas holiday, we made it official and became engaged. I was a little surprised, but I wouldn't say that I was totally surprised. Our relationship had been an attraction of opposites right from the start. Roy was an extrovert who never met a stranger he didn't know. He had the gift of gab and a charming personality to match. I was the exact opposite. Aside from my adventurous streak, I was serious, reserved, and guarded with strangers.

Christmas in Houston was just what I needed to make me feel whole again. I soaked up the warm climate and the loving embrace of Roy and his family. We attended family Christmas celebrations and watched a lot of football on New Year's Day. Life couldn't get any better—if only I didn't have to return to frigid Boston and Harvard. I stayed in Houston for as long as I could and flew back just in time to make my first class for the second semester.

Before I left, Roy and I made a plan that would get us through our separation. He would remain in Houston until the spring and then move to Washington, D.C., where he would set up house and find a job. I would join him after school ended for the summer. For all the romantic novels that I had read as a young girl, you'd think I would have been a crazy, cockeyed romantic, but that wasn't my style. My feet were planted firmly on the ground. Besides, we were mature adults: I was almost twenty-eight and Roy was thirty-five.

When I arrived back at Harvard as an engaged woman, two of my classmates, Carolyn and Nancy, were not surprised when I showed them my ring. As I had gradually opened up to them, I had shared my growing feelings toward Roy. I didn't rush out to tell the others, but as more and more women heard the news, more best wishes came my way. Had I felt closer to my female classmates, my engagement would probably have been an occasion for celebration, but as I have already said, I felt like a stranger to most of them. Nevertheless, in some odd but important way, being engaged changed me: it boosted my self-esteem. I finally "belonged" to someone, and soon I would have a place to call my home. Planning a wedding and building a life with my husband-to-be offered a much-needed respite from the daily struggles I faced at HBS.

*   *   *

By January 1968, the racial tension in this country was explosive. Riots swept across many cities: Atlanta, San Francisco, Oakland, Baltimore, Seattle, Cleveland, Cincinnati, Columbus, Newark, Chicago, New York City, and Detroit. The civil rights movement, led by Dr. Martin Luther King Jr., had become factionalized between pacifists and militant blacks. By 1968, the Black Power movement, which had been gaining momentum since 1966, had overshadowed Dr. King's goal of achieving racial integration through nonviolence. The movement coined the term *black pride* and raised the rhetoric of the Black Panthers, a group that preached equality "by any means necessary."

In this climate, we five black students were prepared to move forward with our mission to increase the black student population. Early in the second semester, we traveled at Harvard's expense to historically black colleges: Morehouse College for men and Spelman College for women (both in Atlanta) as well as Howard University; each of us returned to his or her alma mater to speak to black students about applying to HBS.

Roy Willis and Clif also went to some predominantly white campuses like Stanford University, San Francisco State University, and the University of California at Berkeley, where their efforts produced two recruits. I ended up recruiting two students from Howard. Among the five of us, we recruited many prospective students, twenty-seven of whom enrolled in the class of 1970. This represented a whopping 450 percent increase in the black student population. We had shown the B-School that we knew where and how to find qualified black students.

While we were working to improve race relations at the business school, some white students began to take notice. In the February 8 and 15, 1968, special editions of the *HarBus News,* two white students published the results of a study they had conducted the previous December that dealt with the racial attitudes, policies, and problems of people connected to HBS. The authors, Ben Compaine and John Russell, penned a two-part article titled "The Negro at HBS." The subhead of the first article was "We Come Away Shocked!" The article said the following:

We come away realizing that under our noses are examples of bigotry, discrimination, and apathy. We come away from this project with the saddening knowledge that our Negro alumni and fellow students have in the past been the object of frustrating, deadening discrimination. We see that at the present, the situation is deplorable but that it's changing rapidly—with this change due in part to the business community's programs. We look to the future and feel that the Business School may not be doing enough to implement necessary change and inevitable change.

The second article's subtitle was "Unless We Take the Lead!" The article concluded:

> We can think of no better way of concluding this supplement than to echo the words of FORTUNE [magazine]. "If we are really looking at business to provide leadership in the cities, what may be needed most of all . . . is simply some new attitudes. It is a change already taking place in a good many business communities: Its main feeling is a suddenly intense feeling of involvement with the city on the part of businessmen." It is the same sense of involvement which we feel could be more fully developed at the Harvard Business School.

When these articles were brought to my attention many years later, what I found most interesting was that even though these two students interviewed first-year "Negro" students, they failed to interview the only Negro woman at the school at that time. Could it be that they were not aware that I existed?

*   *   *

One cold February night in 1968, while I was working at the dormitory switchboard, I answered the phone in my usual manner: "Good evening, Radcliffe Graduate Dorm." I immediately recognized the voice on the other end as that of my half brother, Henry, as he said, "Good evening. May I speak to Lillian Hobson?" After I responded, "This is Lillian," there was a deafening silence.

Henry cleared his throat and informed me that Papa had passed away that afternoon. He had had a heart attack while he was sitting in a chair. My father had been in the hospital for about a week with a non-life-threatening illness. Only the day before my mother had assured me that Pa would be coming home soon and not to worry. I had trusted Mama's judgment. Filled with remorse for not having gone home for Christmas, I lowered my head into my hands and began to cry.

The resident manager came to my rescue and relieved me from the switchboard. It was not long before Nancy and Carolyn knocked on my dorm room door. I don't know what I would have done without their loving support. They rallied around me and helped me to pack my bag and make an airline reservation to Virginia to attend the funeral. Nancy drove me to the airport the next day.

When I arrived home, I was consumed with grief and worry. It was the first time that I had seriously thought about dropping out of school. My father's death intensified the loneliness, isolation, and estrangement that I continued to feel at Harvard. Then there was my mother: I couldn't bear the thought of her living alone, especially since she didn't know how to drive. My brothers and I approached Mama and expressed our concern, hoping that she would agree to stay with one of my brothers for a while. She would have none of this fretting, however. She reasoned that she wanted to stay put so she could adjust to being alone. That was typical Mama: strong, practical, and self-sufficient.

My brothers left soon after the funeral, promising to keep a close eye on Mother, but I stayed behind for a few days to comfort and tend to her needs. Although I'm not known for my comic stunts, I did coax a reassuring smile out of my mother when I helped her to run some errands. Papa had a ten-year-old car with a standard transmission. Having never learned how to drive a stick shift, I thought this was as good a time as any to learn. I was a bit nervous, but I rationalized that most of the driving would take place on the unpaved country road, so I was sure that I would get the hang of operating a stick shift before we got to the main highway. As we jerked to and fro, however, I was becoming less patient and more scared, muttering under my breath that I hoped we wouldn't end up with whiplash. God bless my mother: she sat silently and patiently in the passenger seat with an unconcerned countenance. I could almost hear her thinking, *If Lillian says she can drive this clunker, I know she'll do it.*

My flight back to Boston a few days later was as frightening as my stick-shift driving experience was comical. I took the Greyhound bus to Richmond, where my brother Willie John met me at the station to drive me to the airport. A heavy snowstorm had delayed my flight to New York, where I was scheduled to get a connecting flight to Boston. When I landed at LaGuardia Airport, I barely had a moment to catch my breath, much less my flight. I was running down the ramp as the stewardess waved frantically for me to hurry up. As soon as I boarded the plane, the door slammed shut behind me.

I flopped down in my seat and tried to calm my jittery nerves as I stared out the window. Never in my life had I seen so many snowflakes; huge, saucerlike flakes were quickly covering the plane. I had never flown in a snowstorm, and everything about the flight made me feel uneasy. I did the only thing I could: I prayed for a safe takeoff, and I prayed intermittently during the flight. My prayers must have been answered because the flight wasn't as turbulent as I had expected it to be. It was a great relief when the stewardess announced that we were making our descent into Boston, and I said a prayer of thanksgiving for a safe landing.

My feeling of a safe arrival was premature, however. Just as the plane touched down on the runway of Logan Airport, I felt a bumpy movement and realized that we were in serious trouble. The plane skidded, bounced, and came to a screeching halt in a field. There was sheer pandemonium as passengers began scream-ing and clutching one another. I was nervous but remained in my seat, looking out the window to see what was happening.

As soon as the plane stopped, we were herded to the rear exit. All you could hear were the sounds of sirens. There were fire trucks, ambulances, and police cars everywhere. I nearly fainted when I got off the plane and turned around. The nose of the plane was hanging over Boston Harbor! I shuddered to think how close to death we had come—and then I thought how awful it would have been for my family to receive news, so close to the death of my father, that I had died in a plane crash.

Nancy and Carolyn were at the airport waiting for me. They had heard about the harrowing flight but were stunned by my blow-by-blow account.

That night I said "Thank you, God" many times.

*   *   *

Sometime in March the doldrums set in again, and I began to have the same uneasy feeling that had overwhelmed me right before Thanksgiving. I was at my lowest ebb, unsure that I would make it through business school despite all my good intentions and reserves of determination. I wanted out of this godforsaken place in the worst way and began having obsessive thoughts about how I could leave and still save face. That's when an idea came to me.

My professor who taught "Human Behavior in Organizations" had always been pleasant, always making an effort to engage me in conversation. Feeling comfortable in his presence, I decided to make an appointment to talk with him. On the appointed day, I sat down in his office and began to explain my situation. I told him that my father had recently died and that I was concerned about my mother being home alone. I emphasized that I was sure that my mother needed me because she didn't know how to drive. (My mother had not told me that she needed me, but I thought that this would sound like a good reason to leave school.)

He listened attentively as I took a deep breath and continued: "I'm going to have to drop out of school to take care of her. She really needs me." He was unfazed and responded in a matter-of-fact tone: "Okay, Lillian, if you want to quit, go ahead and quit. I'm sure your mother doesn't *really* need you and is probably doing fine without you. But leave if you want to."

Stunned, I stood up and left his office without saying another word. I was furious. I had expected sympathy, and instead he gave me a cold response. My immediate thought was, *I'm not going to quit. I'll show him!* It turns out that he was not cold-hearted; he was clever. He knew exactly what he was doing, and he knew just how to push my buttons. The key word was *quit*. I didn't see myself as a quitter, and I certainly wasn't going to start being one. That ended any thought I had of dropping out.

*   *   *

Spring finally arrived, and April started out on a mild note, especially considering that this was Boston, where you could expect a snowstorm as late as May. The spring thaw filled me with hope, and I was looking forward to the end of the school year, my upcoming wedding, and a summer with my new husband.

Then on April 4, 1968, my world came crashing down. After the trek from class that day, I had gone directly to my room, skipping dinner. For some reason, I was unusually tired, so I decided to take a nap, which I normally didn't do. I set my clock radio for 7:00 p.m., the time I intended to start my studies. When the alarm went off, I woke up to startling news: Dr. Martin Luther King Jr., had been shot at 6:01 p.m. in Memphis, Tennessee. At 7:05 p.m., he was pronounced dead.

My body went limp as I rose and sat on the edge of the bed. Tears, anger, and confusion welled up inside me. This was more than I could bear. The pain felt like chicken bones caught in my throat. First, we had lost President Kennedy, whom the black community had grown to love and trust for his support of civil rights and racial integration. Now, we had lost our most cherished black leader, whose efforts were beginning to bear fruit, or so it seemed. This was in addition to the death of my father—my personal hero who had done all he could to provide for his family.

Glued to my radio, I was anxious to hear any news about the assassination, but I didn't have the strength or the desire to venture out of my room. Although I had a good relationship with Nancy and Carolyn, I had no idea what they thought about Martin Luther King, nor did I know where they stood on civil rights. These were issues we never discussed, and now was not the time to broach the subject. No one knocked on my door that night to see how I was doing. I was engulfed in a deep void as I cried myself to sleep.

The next day I was anxious to participate in a class discussion about Dr. King that I was certain would occur. On my way across the bridge, I was actually thinking of topics and questions to raise. How naive I was. There was no discussion in Section D about Dr. King or his assassination. This was the B-School, after all. Thinking back to this moment, I now regret the lost opportunity. What a difference it could have made had we, myself included, had the nerve to stop what we were doing and address the racial divide, right there in the class-room. It could have been a valuable teaching moment for all of us.

I was later surprised to find out that Roy's section class-mates tried to comfort Roy. Many of them gathered around him and expressed their sympathy, suggesting that he take the day off. He followed their advice and went to Roxbury, the heart of Boston's black community.

It's curious that Roy decided to go on campus that morning. This was the man who said that "every day I made a decision about where I wanted to be. Some days I would go to class; other days I would go to Roxbury to support my brothers." I have to wonder whether he was testing his classmates, to see whether anyone even cared about what had just happened. Roy had undoubtedly devel-oped a different relationship with his classmates than I had. He was vocal, and I'm sure his stance on racial issues was well known.

Clif also opted out of attending class that day. Instead, he, along with his girlfriend and a white student in his section, went to Roxbury to attend a church service. A few days later, having received a loan from a friend, he booked a flight to Atlanta to attend a memorial service for Dr. King at the historic Ebenezer Baptist Church, where Dr. King had been a pastor.

Much to my surprise, classes were canceled on Tuesday, April 9, the day of King's funeral. Many of the women from the dorm and I watched the funeral services on television in the dorm lounge. I can still see the face of Dr. King's widow, Coretta Scott

King. Although she was outwardly composed, her eyes expressed a deep, resigned suffering. She gathered up her four young children and held them close to her. What they didn't understand then, they would understand in time.

Meanwhile, the atmosphere in Harvard Yard—the heart of Harvard University—was dark and foreboding as grief-stricken students gathered to attend memorial services in honor of Dr. King. I learned later that two services were held the day of Dr. King's funeral, one inside Memorial Church (in Harvard Yard) and one outside on the church steps. The latter service was conducted by Harvard University's Association of African and Afro-American Students, known simply as Afro.

Only a month before, Afro had played a key role in having Dr. King invited as the university's commencement speaker in June. His topic was to have been "Asian [Vietnam] Conflict and Urban Crisis." Now Dr. King was gone, and Afro members channeled their anger toward the Harvard administration. On April 10, the day after the funeral, Afro published an ad in the *Harvard Crimson,* the university's student paper, calling for the university to establish an endowed chair for a black professor; offer courses relevant to blacks at Harvard; hire junior-level black faculty members; and admit black students proportionate to their percentage in the population as a whole.

In subsequent weeks, the organization helped to found the Ad Hoc Committee of Black Students to represent black concerns to the Harvard administration. Anger and protests reached a crescendo when a week after the assassination, Harvard University students occupied University Hall, demanding that the university sever its connection with the business school. At this point, the B-School was considered by the demonstrators to be what they called a fascist trade school and feeder of the military-industrial complex.

It's unfortunate that it took a national tragedy to spur the B-School to action. After King's assassination, Roy and Clif intensified their meetings with Dean Baker, who finally acknowledged that he now understood the full scope of the black students' plight. He admitted that the school should play a leadership role, not only to diversify the student body and faculty but also to address urban issues outside Harvard.

With Dean Baker's active support, Roy and Clif pushed for a number of initiatives that included hiring the first black professor, Ulric St. Clair Haynes Jr., as a visiting professor; creating a course entitled "Organizational Development in the Inner City"; forming Boston's first black bank; forming the Urban National Corp, the first major black-oriented equity firm; and creating the Council for Opportunity for Graduate Management Education, which was a consortium of leading business schools specifically designed to recruit and provide financial assistance to minority MBA students.

In addition, the administration gave us black students its blessing in our efforts to create the African American Student Union (AASU), which would become our ultimate contribution to the advancement of black students at the B-School. Over time, AASU would come to symbolize a safe haven for black students. No longer would they feel isolated among their white peers. They would have a place of their own.

That May, my focus was as much on my personal life as it was on my studies and the protests at Harvard and outside the university. In just about six weeks, I would be getting married. I have no idea how I managed to plan a wedding while I was struggling to survive at Harvard. All I knew was that I needed a time-out from a world that was spiraling out of control.

CHAPTER

6

Harvard Business School: 1968–1969

*It is only through labor and painful effort, by grim energy
and resolute courage, that we move on to better things.*

—Theodore Roosevelt

I don't know what I would have done without my adopted mother, Mrs. Hawkins, my landlady from my sophomore year at Howard University. While I was finishing up my first year at Harvard Business School, she attended to every detail of my wedding as if she were planning her own daughter's wedding. She orchestrated the church ceremony, ordered the wedding cake, and made accommodation arrangements for out-of-town guests.

By the time I arrived in D.C., there was nothing left for me to do but be the bride. After the groom, the bridal gown is what every bride falls in love with most. I loved my beautiful white gown with lace trim and a short train. It made me feel elegant and feminine, which was quite a change from the young girl who had to wear Mama's homemade clothes made from burlap bags. Roy and I were married on June 8, 1968, with a small gathering of family and friends by our sides.

Although the ceremony was a blur, I made sure that the word *obey* was not in our otherwise traditional vows. It's not that I didn't respect Roy Lincoln, I just didn't see the point of having to obey my husband, especially if it was against my will. This was the late 1960s, and perhaps I was influenced by the burgeoning feminist movement. Fortunately, Roy didn't have a problem with it.

The day after our wedding, we settled into our two-bedroom apartment in Landover, Maryland, in the same apartment complex where my good friend Anna from the Peace Corps lived. In my absence, she had befriended Roy, helping him to find an apartment and showing him the ins and outs of the neighborhood. There wasn't any point in discussing a honeymoon, since I was knee-deep in student loans—both my Howard loans, which had been deferred during my graduate studies, and my Harvard loans.

At that time, Harvard tuition with room and board was about $5,000 a year. The B-School was already having its effect on me because I was well aware of our balance sheet (assets, liabilities, and net worth), and, believe me, our net worth wasn't much. So instead of going on a honeymoon, Roy took a few days off from his new job as an accountant with the National Labor Relations Board and I took a week off before starting my paid summer internship as a marketing analyst at Humble Oil in Towson, Maryland.

That summer was a delightful diversion from HBS. I reveled in my new role as a newlywed, and I loved fussing around the house, decorating our apartment and whipping up home-cooked meals. I also had a chance to rekindle my friendships with Anna and Vivian (my friend from the Veterans Administration typing pool). We didn't miss a beat. Anna and I picked up from the good old days when I looked for any opportunity and excuse to leave my Howard dorm room to spend the weekend with her. Vivian now had a daughter, and it was exciting to see her in the role of mother.

Despite the long daily commute, I enjoyed my summer job. Roy adjusted to life in the suburbs, and he too liked his new job. All was well with us that summer, although the days went by far too quickly.

When the time came for me to return to school, Roy and I had a mature and rational discussion about the separation period. Nine months apart did not seem like such a long time when we broke it down into segments. We had my school Thanksgiving, Christmas, and spring vacations to look forward to, with the hope that I would be able to squeeze in a long weekend or two in between. We also fantasized, ever so briefly, about the possibility of Roy visiting me in Boston, but we quickly dismissed that idea when we realized that travel and accommodation costs would make it prohibitive. Besides, I knew very little about the city of Boston, and I wouldn't have a clue about where to take Roy and how to entertain him. When I went off campus, it was basically to visit Trish. I guess Harvard had squelched my adventurous spirit, at least temporarily.

I was sad to leave my home, my husband, and my dear friends Anna and Vivian, but I can honestly say that I was excited about returning as a second-year student. Perhaps it was because of my status as a married woman, but I felt completely different from the woman who only a year ago had thrown herself on a park bench in despair. I'm sure that spending the summer with my husband and my friends had helped to restore my confidence, and I was finally beginning to feel like my old self by the time I went back to Harvard. Over the summer, I had had a chance to reclaim the confident, indomitable spirit of the young woman who had been unfazed by many of the challenges that she had already met and conquered in her life.

I had much to look forward to that fall. High on my list was welcoming twenty-seven new black faces on campus, including one woman. In terms of my studies, I knew that the worst was over. I had taken all the required courses and was free to take electives, which I hoped would be easier and more inspiring than my first-year courses. The real source of my confidence, however, lay in the knowledge that there was no question that I would graduate from Harvard with an MBA. I was halfway through, and nothing was going to stop me now.

*   *   *

If Harvard taught me one thing—and believe me, it taught me many things—it was that dissatisfaction with the status quo can lead to change if you channel your discontent and work from inside the system to change it. That the efforts of a group of five first-year black students had improved the school's recruitment of blacks showed me that change was indeed possible—even at an institution like Harvard where the status quo does not change easily. That fall I was very proud of our accomplishment.

The concept for the black student organization on campus, the African American Student Union (AASU), had emerged during Roy (Willis) and Clif's recruitment visit the preceding spring to the University of California at Berkeley. They had an opportunity to meet with the president of UC-Berkeley's Afro-American Student Union and were impressed with the organization's mission and initiatives.

Roy was emphatic about the need to establish a similar organization at Harvard. How right he was to understand that it was not enough to recruit black students and set them loose in a hostile environment to fight for their own survival. He saw very clearly that we needed to provide a safety net to ensure that black students would not only survive but actually thrive at Harvard. What good would it have been if incoming black students were destined for the same fractured, isolated, and lonely existence that typified our experiences?

A vision without a plan is only a pipe dream, so Clif made sure that the new organization was rooted in reality. He had remained in Boston the previous summer, laying the groundwork for the organization. He also served as the main point of contact for incoming black students, answering questions and gathering and sharing information about the class of 1969's efforts to make the school more accommodating to black students. As the liaison, he disseminated information about the formation of

AASU, and he encouraged the first-year students to join with the second-year students in the fall in the spirit of solidarity.

The framework of AASU was revealed when Roy and Trish hosted a fall orientation party in their home for the black students of the classes of 1969 and 1970. Fall orientation for black students would evolve into a more formal and elaborate welcome in subsequent years, but there was something special about our first annual orientation. We embraced our new recruits as if they were precious gems that we were coddling in our hands.

I'll never forget our first gathering. Taking command as the host, Roy turned off the music that had been playing, and the atmosphere in the room turned from lighthearted conversation to absolute quiet. All eyes were on him. He started off in a modulated tone, telling the incoming students that we were glad they had chosen the B-School and that Harvard had much to offer if they studied hard and applied themselves. Then, like a preacher delivering a God-inspired homily, he raised his voice and spoke eloquently.

The gist of his speech was that he urged the incoming black students to commit to an ethos of giving back to our communities and not distance themselves from black issues or black people outside Harvard. He went on to say that this was the commitment that the second-year students had made and he hoped (or rather expected) the first-year students to carry on the example and legacy that we were attempting to establish.

The response from the first-year students was overwhelmingly positive. The black student body bonded at that moment, and AASU came to life at Harvard Business School.

Clif spoke next and described the various subcommittees he had worked so hard on creating over the summer. Each committee was designed to focus on a major area of interest to black students. To ensure that our organization had the resources to pursue its endeavors, students were asked to direct their obligatory student association dues to our organization instead of to the officially recognized student association. Unfortunately, this request later caused quite a stir when word got out to the leaders of the school's officially recognized student association. They confronted the administration and demanded that black students be forced to pay dues to the association like everyone else on campus. Clif appealed to a sympathetic professor who interceded on our behalf to resolve the issue. The dues problem never came up again.

After the formal speeches, the atmosphere turned soulful as the "veterans" told their "war stories." My story struck a chord when I spoke about the isolation I felt as the lone black woman. I shared with the group how intimidated I had been about speaking up in class, but I stressed the importance of class participation because it accounted for a large percentage of one's grade.

Collectively and individually, we emphasized our commitment to fortify and empower the black student community, which was still fragile and vulnerable. We buoyed the new students' spirits by telling them that they were just as competent, talented, and smart as their white counterparts. We also warned them that they would be put to the test to see if they could measure up and make the grade.

All this talk about excelling and measuring up made me reflect on my days growing up in the South, when black children were always told that we had to be twice as good to compete in white society. After my Harvard experience—where the crème de la crème of white society floats to the top—I would definitely have to say that black students at Harvard still have to be better than their white counterparts to compete.

In contrast to our humble gathering, today's black orientations welcome the first-year students with pomp and ceremony. The orientation begins with an informal barbecue, which typically takes place in a second-year student's residence and is not unlike that first gathering of 1968. A few days later, a formal reception is held on campus for the B-School's entire black community: faculty, staff, students, and alumni. The orientation culminates with a weekend retreat in a picturesque location, where both first- and second-year students have an opportunity to bond and hang out together in a relaxed setting away from campus before they have to crack open the books. I was touched to hear a recent student reflect the spirit of the organization when she remarked that "AASU is a home away from home." Amen!

AASU also hosts an annual conference in Boston during the second semester that is attended by hundreds of students, prospective students, alumni, and corporations. Today's black students and many alumni may not be aware that this annual conference dates back to 1970, when the members of the class of 1970 surprised the members of the class of 1969 with a gathering of thanksgiving to express their appreciation for all that had been done for them and for future classes of black students. In 2002, the annual conference was named the H. Naylor Fitzhugh Conference in honor of my mentor and HBS alumnus.

*   *   *

The B-School must have done a heck of a job breaking me down and building me up in my first year because my second-year course load seemed a lot more manageable. Then again, perhaps it was because I could see the light at the end of the tunnel. It wouldn't be long before my academic career would be behind me. It was a pleasure taking a course that my classmates Roy and Clif had been responsible for introducing into the curriculum, "Organization Development in the Inner City." It's hard to believe that this bastion of conservative thinking had conceded to offer such a course, but the fact that it did was proof that the black students were leaving their mark on the school.

In my second year, I also went beyond the confines of the campus, a sure sign that my adventurous spirit had not been squelched after all. I successfully secured a part-time job with Sterling Institute, a consulting firm in Boston that specialized in contracts with a federal government agency, the Office of Economic Opportunity (OEO). The agency had been created in August 1964 as part of President Lyndon Johnson's social and economic initiatives known as the Great Society and the War on Poverty. As a contractor to the OEO, Sterling performed work that coincided with my own desire to improve the status and living conditions of America's poor.

That spring, the campus was flooded with recruiters who were eager to scoop up the proverbial best and brightest. At the time, management consulting and investment banking were all the rage. If you landed a job with McKinsey & Company, for instance, you were on the road to wealth, power, and influence. Since I was going back to Maryland to reunite with my husband, I chose not to sign up with any recruiters. Besides, Sterling Institute had offered me a position in its D.C. office. This did not change the fact that I was acutely aware that I was not sought out by recruiters the way many of my classmates were. It became obvious to me that the desirable students were courted and feted by recruiters from blue-chip companies. When I stopped to think of my own situation, I knew I presented a problem. What would corporate America do in 1969 with a black woman, even if she did have a Harvard MBA? I was too much of a risk, too much of an anomaly, too much of an enigma.

Apparently, I wasn't the only one who felt left out in the cold in corporate America. My classmate Robin shared with me a poem that she wrote for our twenty-fifth HBS reunion. "The Road to Wisdom" expressed her view of the attitude of corporate America toward women in our era.

> Left HBS eager, all full of hope,
> Terribly naive, ill-prepared to cope.
> Business was not ready for women in our day.
> Limited our choices, affecting our pay.

I really can't say if the black male students were actively recruited, but I am pretty sure that they were not at the top of the recruitment list, given the composition of corporate America at the time. I do know this: Clif remained at HBS to work on his doctorate. Roy started a small business in California. Ted accepted a position with a job placement firm in New York. George did not return to complete his degree with his class but came back and finished with the class of 1970. No one knows what happened to Carlson.

*   *   *

My marriage survived my time at Harvard quite well. In fact, I think being at Harvard may have strengthened it. Although my husband and I didn't see each other much except for holidays and occasional weekends, we considered the time we spent together to be precious. Thus, we didn't dwell on petty issues that typically arise when a newly married couple is adjusting to each other and married life.

Anticipating my graduation on June 12, Mom and my husband, Roy, could barely contain their excitement; they kept telling me that they couldn't wait to see me receive my degree. I, however, was not at all excited, and for a split second I gave some thought to skipping the graduation ceremony. Even though the second year had been a lot better than the first year, I just wanted to leave Harvard and get on with my life. Nevertheless, I felt a responsibility to my strongest supporters—my mother and Roy—and didn't have the heart to deprive them of this special moment.

The sun shone brightly that day as thousands of people—a pretty distinguished crowd, I might add—milled about. I thought back to graduation day at Howard and how proud I had been to look out and see my family, my relatives, and my friends cheering me on. Compared to the B-School's graduation, Howard's graduation had seemed like a great big family reunion, with people hugging, kissing, talking, and smiling. This was not the case with my Harvard graduation.

I concluded that HBS's graduation existed primarily for its white population. The code of elitism was clearly evident as well-heeled parents and friends nodded, shook hands, and spoke in muffled tones to one another. Even on the last day on B-School soil, many of the black students felt out of place. Breaking through the color barrier exacts a price. There were still some hard feelings because there had not been enough time to heal the wounds. One or two black students even opted out of the graduation ceremony. Roy Willis, who had done so much to improve the status of black students, chose not to attend because he did not consider a Harvard graduation a celebration.

I was there in body but not in spirit: even though I had become more confident in my second year, I regressed at that moment. Emotions that had overwhelmed me on my first day on campus now resurfaced. I thought back to the girl on the park bench. She was older and wiser, but she was also more wary. Here I was among all these white students who were enthusiastically looking to venture out into the corporate world, many certain of their future. Not I, however; nothing was for certain.

Only as we were driving back to Maryland did it hit me that I, Lillian Lincoln, had just received my MBA from Harvard! My euphoria quickly dissolved, however, and was replaced with many burning, unsettling questions: *What would this degree do for me? Could I really make a difference working at the Sterling Institute for inner city initiatives?* My thoughts turned dark as I began to examine the implications of my newly minted Harvard MBA degree. I knew that many people in the outside world saw Harvard graduates as being elitist and self-righteous, and I wondered if I would be viewed the same way. But most important, I wondered how I would be perceived by my family, friends, and colleagues.

It was a fact that I was entering uncharted territory. There was no one out there like me—a black woman with an MBA from Harvard. I wondered if this would change me as a person. I knew I had to walk a tightrope and balance myself between two worlds: the world of my contemporaries who had advanced degrees and good-paying jobs and the world of my friends and family—the people in Ballsville, Riverhead, and New York City—many of whom had no college degrees but who had advanced degrees in living.

As reality set in, I made a vow to keep this degree in perspective and not let it swell my head. I vowed to remain humble and never forget my roots. The ride home was sobering. Little did my mother and Roy know what was going through my head.

Arnetha B. Hobson (1922). Mom's official graduation portrait from Virginia Normal and Industrial Institute. This picture shows her beautiful head of hair, which I always admired.

Mom's parents (about 1950). Grandpa and Grandma, John and Hattie Hobson, dressed in their Sunday finery.

Weldon Hobson (1951). My brother with his pride and joy—his 1937 Plymouth—in front of our Ballsville home. This is the red clay road I talked about.

Willie D. Hobson (about 1960). Pa dressed in his Sunday best after attending a special function.

H. Naylor Fitzhugh
(about 1965). My professor
and mentor at Howard
University who changed the
course of my life by telling
me that I deserved to go to
Harvard Business School.

Willie D. Hobson (1966).
Pa at the dining room table
in his usual and his most
comfortable attire—his
work clothes.

I'm all smiles on the front steps of Mrs. Hawkins's house in my cap and gown after graduating from Howard University in May of 1966.

Here I am on graduation day from Harvard Business School in June of 1969.

My official graduation photo as it appeared in the 1969 Harvard Business School yearbook.

Rudolph (Rudy) DePass (1971). My cousin pestered me to go to college. His nagging paid off. Here he's sitting in his office at the University of Maryland, where he was a graduate student.

Mom surrounded by her children—(from left to right) Willie John, me, Clyde, Hattie, Henry, and Weldon—on her eightieth birthday in November of 1979.

7

Life beyond Harvard

Allowing the truth of who you are—your spiritual self—to rule your life means you stop the struggle and learn to move with the flow of your life.

—Oprah Winfrey

With my newly minted MBA and a head full of idealism, I was eager to embark on my brilliant career. My job with Sterling Institute's War on Poverty program was waiting for me when I returned to Washington, D.C. There were a few times in my budding career when being a black person was not only advantageous but also necessary. This job was one of them.

As an associate, I was hired to work with community action agencies to train community organizers who were assigned to go into impoverished neighborhoods to teach poor residents, most of whom were black, job skills that would help them to become gainfully employed. Since I had grown up in the type of rural neighborhood that the agencies were servicing, my boss saw me as a person who would be able to establish a rapport with the trainers, many of whom were also black.

My boss was right. As liberal and compassionate as he was, he was a white man in his mid-forties, and it wasn't easy for him to gain the trust and acceptance of the participants. Most southern blacks were suspicious of white outsiders coming into their communities. The Civil War had been won, segregation had been outlawed, and reform legislation had been created to address poverty and social inequities, yet the racial divide was still what it had always been: a chasm in the hearts and psyche of the American people.

Unfortunately, after two years, my job at Sterling went the way of the War on Poverty program. Funds dried up, the Washington office closed, and I lost my job. As sometimes happens with federally funded programs, a lot of money was wasted on big salaries, high overhead, impractical strategies, and unrealistic goals. After the initial exhilaration, I had actually found the work and the travel depressing. I used to wonder how on earth we were going to get all these people out of poverty. It was like using a teaspoon to empty the ocean.

Somewhat discouraged but not yet defeated, I was hell-bent on working for social justice. The perfect opportunity came my way with a position at the National Bankers Association. Founded in 1927, the association advocated for banks owned by minorities and women on legislative and regulatory matters that affected its members and the communities they served.

Although I knew about the Industrial Bank of Washington, an old-line minority-owned bank established in 1934 and the oldest bank in the National Bankers Association, I was not aware that there were so many black-owned banks scattered throughout the country. Thus, I saw this job as giving me another opportunity to help improve the conditions of black communities while also exposing me to the world of black business ownership. At least the goals of this organization seemed a lot more practical and achievable than those of my previous job.

It certainly didn't hurt that the hiring executive director and I had something in common: we were both Harvard Business School graduates. Dr. Edward Irons, a black man in his early forties, received a doctorate in business administration at HBS in 1960. Just like that, my Harvard degree worked its magic. We connected, and I was hired as his assistant.

This was the first time that I experienced the power of a world-class education. All I had to do was say that I went to

Harvard, and presto, the doors swung open and I was welcomed into the inner sanctum of the business world. In hindsight, I wish that I had taken greater advantage of the Harvard network, which prides itself on taking care of its own, in my efforts to advance my career. However, at that point in my life, fresh out of Harvard, I couldn't reconcile my feelings that even though I had gone to Harvard, I had never felt part of it. It would take decades before I felt that Harvard was a place to which I belonged. I was living W. E. B. DuBois's words: "I was in Harvard, but not of it."

* * *

Life was good on the home front. After a year of apartment living, Roy and I decided that it was time to become homeowners, living the two-income suburbanite life. We looked for houses in all-black neighborhoods, but when we took a closer look at the amenities— or, I should say, lack of amenities—in such communities, they did not meet our standards. Even though I had heard of such discrepancies between white and black neighborhoods, I was stunned to note the marked difference in the quality of town services, such as street maintenance, trash collection, street lighting, and, most important, the caliber of the school systems.

This became evident on one particular house-hunting weekend when we visited a brand-new development that was near completion in a predominantly white neighborhood in Bowie, Maryland. Roy and I were immediately drawn to a split-level house that was under construction. What made it even more attractive was that the houses on both sides of it were already occupied. This was a clear sign that people were buying into the development, which made us think that we were making a good investment.

The sales office provided us with all the information we needed, including the assurance that we could afford the mortgage. With a mixture of excitement and reservation, we took the information home to "sleep on it." It was a bit scary to make such a financial commitment, because the mortgage was twice as much as our rent, but we rationalized that it was time to take the leap and make the American Dream a reality.

Lo and behold, our offer of $37,500 was accepted, and we were the first blacks to move into the neighborhood. I'll never know for sure whether we were trendsetters, but a few black families moved in right after us. Our white neighbors were friendly enough, although at the outset we didn't socialize together. That all changed after our girls were born and a white family who had a daughter the same age as my youngest daughter moved in down the street. Our daughters played together and became long-term friends. It's funny how children can bring adults together. In fact, the girl's mother and I remained friends for several years even after the family moved from the neighborhood.

Less than a year after we settled into our new home, my position at National Bankers Association was no longer funded, and I was out of a job again. So much for job security and working for a noble cause; so much for a career path. At this point, I was disabused of the notion that a career was linear, predictable, progressive, and long lasting. Instead, I was beginning to see it as a series of chutes and ladders.

At least Roy had a secure, reasonably good-paying job as an accountant with the federal government. We had no children, so meeting our financial obligations, though a bit pressing, was not a major issue. Still, for a woman who cherishes her independence, the thought of not working made me feel uncomfortable.

I started scouring the newspapers, and I came across an ad for an investment seminar conducted by Ferris & Company. I had been reading about investments, and this was as good a time as any to broaden my knowledge of the investment world—a world that I knew little about. My folks and I never sat around the dinner table discussing the stock market and our investments, which I imagined many of my Harvard classmates doing. My parents were not investors, and, to my knowledge, neither were my siblings.

This would be uncharted territory, but I was excited by the newness of it. I attended the seminar and found it informative. Moreover, I found it refreshing that a woman was leading the seminar. Gail Winslow, a white woman in her late forties or early fifties, was a dynamic speaker. Answering questions in a thoughtful, intelligent way, she made the subject matter sound fascinating. She had been in the business for a number of years and was one of the company's top producers.

At the end of the session, I approached her to let her know how much I enjoyed her presentation. We started to talk, and she asked me if I had ever considered a career in the brokerage business. When I told her that I had not, she encouraged me to think about it, emphasizing that there were few women in the industry and even fewer black women. She got my full attention when she stressed that I had the potential of making a good living.

It sounded promising. I was not working, and I had no other prospects. Seeing Gail as somewhat of a role model—here was a woman making money in a man's world—I thought that this could be a good opportunity and a great learning experience. Our conversation ended with Gail saying that she would schedule an interview for me with George Ferris Jr., the company's owner and president. If nothing else, I was impressed that she thought that I should meet with the top honcho. However, I think she had something else up her sleeve: she saw me as her protégé, and she wanted me to be brought in by the top guy.

I was pleasantly surprised by what I saw the day of my interview. Although I noticed few female brokers in the office (I counted five), they all seemed pretty sharp. I was especially impressed with another top producer who, I later learned, was a legend in the industry. Julia Walsh, also a white woman, had made a name for herself as a powerful businesswoman in Washington, D.C. She was a woman of many firsts, including the first female governor of the American Stock Exchange, the first female director of the U.S. Chamber of Commerce, the first female president of the Greater Washington Board of Trade, the first female graduate of the Advance Management Program of the Harvard Business School, and the first female business graduate from the Kent State University College of Business.

I also learned that day that Ferris & Company was an anomaly in the financial arena: it employed more women than any other brokerage firm did at the time. However, they were all white women.

My interview with the president went well, and he seemed genuinely supportive of women. However, during the interview, he made a comment that troubled me. He said that white clients would welcome me as their broker because they "could relate it to [my] being a servant to them." I thought it was an absurd remark—I knew of no instance in which servants gave financial advice or handled money for their employers. Nevertheless, I let the comment pass. I was hired as an account executive in the fall of 1971. The job was a refreshing change from the nonprofit sector and a series of dead-end, federally funded jobs.

After going through a short training program to learn the basics of the business—how the stock market functions, how orders are transacted, and how commissions are structured—I was eager to settle into my job. Much to my chagrin, however, I soon learned that I had neither the personality nor the network to develop the client base necessary to make a decent income. It also didn't help that I came into the business near the height of a bull market that soon after my arrival devolved into a bear market. I thought, *I have taken on some challenges in my career, but this may be the ultimate. I'm paid only if I sell.*

Although the title *stockbroker* sounded impressive, I came to understand that I was really nothing more than a glorified saleswoman who had to make cold calls. I recalled my days of selling magazine subscriptions. This job was no different, except that I had the luxury of making sales calls from behind a desk instead of hitting the streets, going door-to-door. Thank God for small comforts.

My thoughts quickly turned to my role models, Gail and Julia, and I wondered how they built their client base. It was time to have a conversation with Gail and learn the secret of how she got her start in the business. Her answer was simple but startling: "I started with my own contacts—friends, family, and business associates." Bells went off in my head. There were too many things wrong with this job. I didn't have a network of wealthy prospects, and I didn't have a clue about how to build a network of wealthy clients. Furthermore, I hated making cold calls, and I wasn't comfortable recommending investments based on my limited knowledge of how stocks performed.

What really got to me, however, was the way we made our commissions: we were frequently encouraged to push the investments that paid the highest commissions—that is, in-house stocks—and were therefore the most profitable to the firm. Therein lay a moral dilemma: my recommendation was not always the best recommendation for my client. This was an unconscionable conflict of interest.

No sooner did I decide that I would have to look for another job than I discovered that I was pregnant with my first child. I was earning little money, but this was not the time to leave a job, especially now with a child on the way.

Roy and I had not discussed when we would have children, and I was so busy trying to build a career that I had not given it much thought. But Roy's excitement about having a baby made me excited; yet, like most working-parents-to-be, we suddenly came face-to-face with the child-care issue. Fortunately, the issue miraculously resolved itself the day I got a call from my mother.

It had been just over three years since Pa died. While my mother steeled herself for cold winters by huddling close to a wood-burning stove and endured hot summers with only a hand fan offering some relief, I think she was finding life on the farm to be a challenge, especially at her age—she was seventy-two years old. I had always made it clear that when she was ready to leave the farm that she would be welcome to live with us. As soon as she heard that I was pregnant, she made up her mind. The timing couldn't have been better. She moved in right before the baby was born. What better person to watch over our new baby than my loving mother.

*   *   *

With the child-care issue resolved, I now had to confront my work situation. Many companies, especially in the financial world, were just getting used to the idea of hiring professional women, so I was very concerned about how I would be seen as a pregnant professional woman. At that time, it was not yet illegal to ask a female job applicant if she intended to become pregnant or to fire a female employee when she became pregnant. Even though pregnant workers today are protected under the law, many women still agonize over how and when to break the news to their employers that they are pregnant, for fear that they will be relegated to the "mommy track." Although the situation has improved since my time, we haven't come far enough: women in the twenty-first century still face an uncertain future in having children and maintaining a career at the same time. I was not looking forward to telling my employer that I was pregnant, but I need not have worried: Ferris & Company considered it a nonissue, which was highly radical for the time.

I had an easy pregnancy—no morning sickness and hardly any weight gain—and I worked right up until the day before I delivered my daughter, Darnetha LaRoi Lincoln, on August 30, 1972. We wanted to name our firstborn daughter after my mother, so I came up with a creative twist on my mother's name, Arnetha, by adding the letter D before her name. Darnetha was an easy baby who cried very little and slept through the night after only a couple of weeks.

After a six-week maternity leave, I returned to Ferris & Company. The sharing in the care of Darnetha was carefully orchestrated. Mother took care of her during the day, and Roy and I shared the evening and night shift according to our personalities.

Roy, like Darnetha, was a night owl, so he was responsible for her midnight feeding. I, the morning person, scooped her up out of the crib at six o'clock, bathed her, fed her, and turned her over to Mother before leaving for work.

My home life was as satisfying as my career was unsatisfying. I was determined to give Ferris my best shot, but my heart just wasn't in it. In less than four years out of business school, I was about to look for my fourth job. One glance at my sketchy résumé was enough for me to realize that I was missing the mark. It was depressing to know that even with a Harvard MBA, I was having a hard time finding my niche.

Since I hadn't maintained contact with any of my female classmates at Harvard, I had no way of knowing whether they too were finding it hard to establish a career path. It was only decades later that I had an opportunity to speak with one of the women from my class, and I learned that she had found corporate America to be a hard climb. She confided in me that although Harvard had given her the critical-thinking and leadership skills to excel in the business world, she could never master the political game in her efforts to make partner in her company.

I decided to try my hand at higher education. What did I have to lose? I applied for a teaching position at Bowie State College and received an offer, which I accepted. I resigned from Ferris & Company in time to take the summer off. Darnetha was just about nine months old, and I was looking forward to spending time with her. That summer I learned a lot about myself, including that while I loved Darnetha and being a mother, I missed the business world. I was not cut out to be a stay-at-home mother.

Like many mothers, I questioned whether there was something wrong with me for wanting to go back to work. I had always wanted to be independent and self-sufficient, so being a career woman felt natural. I had to retrain myself not to feel guilty about wanting to have a career and a family. Today, when my daughters and other young women talk to me about the mother-versus-career dilemma, I always tell them that it's an individual choice and that there are no right or wrong answers. My advice to women is that they have to be comfortable with their decision and not feel guilty about the choices they make.

However, I was in for a big surprise. It was July, and I discovered that I was pregnant with my second child. This pushed me over the edge. I had a crying spell because I couldn't believe the untimeliness of this situation. Darnetha was not even out of diapers, and a second baby was on the way. I knew that this was no way for a loving mother to act, so I rationalized that since Darnetha was such a good baby, my second would surely be the same. However, I had a more serious concern: I had signed a contract to teach in the fall, and I wondered if I would be able to honor it.

Like most modern couples who struggle to balance work and family issues, Roy and I discussed our options, and he was comfortable with whatever decision I made. Whether I stayed home or returned to work, our financial situation would be negatively affected because we would have an additional child-care expense or less income. Mom was a great help with Darnetha, but I was becoming increasingly concerned about her ability (given her age) to take care of a toddler and an infant at the same time. This would be asking too much of her. We had only one option: we needed to hire someone to help with child care.

That July I got a call that would change the course of my life forever. On the other end of the phone was Amelia Davis, a woman I had worked with at Sterling Institute. After we exchanged pleasantries, she got right to the point and told me that her dad had a janitorial company and that he needed someone to help him put the company back on track. I was surprised and flattered that Amelia had recommended me to her father. Even though we had worked together on some projects at Sterling, I had no idea that she thought so highly of me. No sooner had I told her that I would be glad to talk to her father than her dad called. After a brief conversation, I agreed to meet with him in his office in downtown D.C.

I liked Jerry Davis immediately. He was a stylish dresser, and he walked with an air of confidence. I learned that he had retired from the army as a lieutenant colonel and that he had grown up in a small town in Louisiana. Even though he had only a high school diploma, I was impressed that he was running his own company. What I liked most about Jerry was that he had a natural talent for making people feel comfortable in his presence. In other words, he was a consummate salesman. My impression of him would deepen over time. But on the surface he seemed to be a happy-go-lucky guy who enjoyed the better things in life. Fine wine and cigars were his trademark. Our meeting clinched the deal: I agreed to work as a consultant until my job at Bowie State started in the fell.

By the end of my first day on the job, my head was spinning. Unified Services, Inc., had every conceivable problem that a small business could have: unpaid withholding taxes (by far the most serious), delinquent bank loans, unpaid vendors, overdue receivables, and other major cash-flow issues. This gave me a glimpse into Jerry's darker side. He had a cavalier, spendthrift attitude about running a business. Whereas some new employees may have been overwhelmed with the magnitude of these problems, these were exactly the kind of challenges that I was seeking. Finally, I would be able to put my hard-earned MBA degree to work.

My first assignment was to disentangle the company's mess with the Internal Revenue Service. After I discussed the issue with Jerry, it became clear to me that other people he had hired before me had attempted to resolve the matter but had only made things worse. Payment arrangements were made and broken, and Unified's survival was at stake.

I had my work cut out for me. The first thing I had to do was to regain the respect and the trust of the IRS agent who was assigned to Jerry's case. My dealings with the IRS proved pivotal for how I would approach business from that day forward. Although my Harvard education had taught me negotiation and accounting skills, I was now beginning to rely more and more on my intuitive abilities in dealing with the human part of business. At the time I attended Harvard Business School, the curriculum did not emphasize human behavior courses because they were considered to be "soft."

Whenever possible, and most especially with serious matters, I would always request a face-to-face meeting with the person with whom I was considering doing business. Nothing beats this kind of communication in terms of what you can learn about people. Not only do you hear their words, you also observe their body language. The way a person approaches you, greets you, and looks at you reveals truths that a telephone voice can always disguise.

The goal of my first meeting with the IRS agent was to gain his trust and establish a rapport by being respectful and gracious. As I explained the company's problems, he listened attentively and appeared to be open minded and cooperative. At the end of our conversation, he confessed that the real source of his anger had been the company's representatives. He told me that they had been rude and condescending and had treated him like a government lackey. I assured him that things would be different with me. After all, this was the man who at a moment's notice could decide the fate of Unified Services. He had my respect. In the end, he proposed that I draw up a payment plan for his consideration.

I returned to the office and made the case for why my boss should give me the authority to negotiate a deal with the IRS. Jerry couldn't have been happier to hand the entire situation over to me. After reviewing the company's financial books, I came up with a realistic payment plan, which I then presented in person to the agent. We negotiated a repayment plan for more than $120,000 plus interest. The agent accepted the proposal, and I kept my promise to make monthly payments over the next two years.

In the first six weeks, I also repaired my boss's relationships with his bankers and vendors. In both cases, I met in person with the concerned parties, won their confidence and trust, and came up with new agreements. With my help, the company's bank loan was restructured and vendor lines of credit were reinstated. A couple of weeks before my consulting agreement was to end, Jerry offered me a full-time job. But as much as I enjoyed working at Unified, I felt obligated to honor my prior commitment to Bowie State. Jerry, however, made a counteroffer that sounded very attractive. He said he would let me work around my teaching job on a part-time basis.

This was a tall order, and I had much to consider. I enjoyed my work and liked my boss very much. We made a good team, and I got along well with his administrative staff and key managers. I also knew that I could make a difference: I had the skills, training, and knowledge that could help the company grow and prosper. Nevertheless, I was concerned about the demands on my time—holding down two jobs while taking care of a toddler and another baby on the way.

After discussing the situation with Roy, I was convinced that it was doable. The extra money was a plus. I accepted Jerry's offer and was hired as executive vice president with responsibilities for all functions, except marketing, which my boss performed masterfully. As I said, his sales skills were next to none.

Unified Services had been founded in 1971 and had experienced rapid growth with the assistance of the Small Business Administration's 8(a) program. The program was a new initiative that was designed specifically to give "disadvantaged" people (defined at that time as blacks) the opportunity to bid on and negotiate government contracts. This initiative was an attempt to redress the unfairness of the procurement and contract selection process, which until that time had been weighted against minority-owned businesses. The main requirement for acceptance into the program was that you had to be black and own at least 51 percent of your business. Some version of this program exists today, although the definition of *disadvantaged* has been expanded to include other ethnic groups.

Under the 8(a) program, Unified Services had been awarded several government contracts that accelerated the company's growth at an uncontrollable rate. By the time I arrived, the company had revenues of approximately $3 million but suffered from severe cash-flow problems and loose internal financial controls. An outside accounting firm was responsible for the year-end financial statements, whereas the day-to-day bookkeeping was handled by an employee whose accounting skills were questionable. Many problems surfaced as a result: invoices were not sent out on a timely basis, and collections were overdue. Questions swirled around in my head: *Who's managing the cash? Who's managing the company? Is this a "lifestyle company" that takes care of the owner first?*

Therein lay another problem. My biggest challenge had nothing to do with the business; it had to do with controlling the boss. He enjoyed spending money not only on himself but on others as well. He took employees and friends out for drinks, lunch, and dinner. He was so generous that he was willing to lend employees money even though some never paid him back.

His American Express card would slip out of his hand like butter sliding off a hot pancake. He never left home without it, as the slogan goes, and he never failed to use it, either. When the bill arrived each month, I'd always sit him down to have a heart-to-heart talk about his excessive spending, but he refused to heed my reprimands. He always agreed with whatever I recommended, but seldom did he live up to our agreement. I also couldn't control my boss's marketing efforts, which usually involved spending money that the company didn't have. I soon learned that although he had a gift for winning new business—it helped that he wined and dined his prospects in style—the company lacked the financial resources to honor the terms of the contracts.

New contracts required about ninety days of working capital to cover start-up costs of payroll, equipment, and supplies. The company was operating so close to the edge that at times the ability to meet payroll was questionable. There always seemed to be a cash-flow crunch. The advantage of winning a government contract was that you were assured of being paid; the disadvantage was that you could not always be sure when you would be paid. Sometimes it could take up to 120 days. For a labor-intensive business, cash availability is critical.

I don't know how I was able to maintain this ungodly workload, holding down two jobs while raising a toddler and being pregnant. All I can say is that my capacity for hard work expanded to meet the demands of my commitments. I taught every weekday at Bowie—a total of four courses—then drove to downtown D.C., arriving at Unified about midday. I came home in time for dinner, around 6:30 p.m.

That first year, juggling two jobs and a toddler was a backbreaking challenge, but I got some much-needed relief in January from my college position. January was considered a compact session in which veteran teachers were required to teach. As a new instructor, I was off the hook. I welcomed the school recess because I needed some rest, particularly since my second baby was due in early February.

The baby, however, had another plan. Tasha Renee Lincoln arrived a month premature, by cesarean section, on January 8, 1974. Weighing four pounds two ounces, she had to stay in the hospital for two weeks until she reached five pounds. Since school was in recess, I spent the month bonding with Tasha and recuperating from the operation.

I could not have had a better boss. When I was able to work, Jerry allowed me to work from home until I felt comfortable going back to the office. His secretary would drop off work at my home, which made it an ideal work arrangement. In this regard, Jerry could be seen as a man ahead of his time, endorsing what would become known in the 1990s workplace as "telecommuting."

*   *   *

During my second semester at Bowie State, I was offered a teaching contract for the following school year; this was at the same time that Jerry offered me a full-time, permanent job. My decision wasn't difficult to make. I enjoyed teaching, but I had no intention of pursuing a doctorate, which is what I would have to do if I were to continue in an academic career. Running a small business suited me better, so I gladly accepted Jerry's offer.

Although the job issue had been resolved, we still had to deal with child care. Even though we didn't consider ourselves well off financially, we were willing to make the sacrifice to hire live-in help. Roy and I came up with a plan whereby Mom would oversee the household and monitor the person who would have the major responsibility for taking care of the girls.

Not knowing quite how to proceed—we had never had live-in help, and we didn't know anyone who had—Roy and I nonetheless developed our own criteria for the position based on our own values and needs. We knew we wanted a black person. We were uncomfortable having a white person caring for our children. We also reasoned that a black person would feel better about working for a black family rather than a white family, which may or may not be true. Most important, we wanted to make sure that this person would accept being supervised by my mother.

We took out an ad in the help-wanted section of the local newspaper, interviewed a few candidates, and settled on a woman named Dottie, who was in her mid-forties. She turned out to be a gentle and loving caretaker, a great cook, and the perfect addition to our family. In fact, soon after she came to live with us, we learned that Dottie had no family in the area or anywhere else. We were her family. Initially, we were concerned about her agility because she was obese, but she moved like a dancing bear. In short, she was a gem who was with us for three years until she had a stroke. She ended up in a nursing home and died a few years later.

After Dottie left, the child-care problem reared its ugly head yet again, but fate intervened. My sister, Hattie, who some years earlier had moved from Richmond to New York, was tired of living in New York and was looking for a change of scenery. I thought, *What a coincidence! I need help and Hattie wants to leave the city.* She had previously worked for families in both domestic and child-care capacities, so this seemed like the perfect solution.

If Mom had any reservations about this arrangement, she kept them to herself. I, on the other hand, chose to overlook Hattie's track record with her own children: she had two boys, neither of whom she raised herself. I succumbed to wishful thinking, hoping that this would give us an opportunity to come together as sisters.

The first year went well, but then I started to notice that Mom was doing most of the caretaking. My mother would certainly never squeal on Hattie—she would never think of pitting sisters against each other—but I was keeping a close eye on Hattie and had observed that she was short tempered, angry, belligerent, and generally miserable. When we finally had a talk, she complained that she was overworked, that she felt mistreated, and that she was made to feel inferior.

I was stunned to hear these accusations because I thought we had done everything to make her feel comfortable. However, when I stopped to think about the situation, I began to understand her feelings. Hattie never finished high school, and here she was taking care of her younger sister's children. It didn't matter that the girls loved her. We finally agreed that she should get her own place and find another job. I felt terrible because I had truly wanted it to work out. I guess I was expecting too much.

By the time Hattie left, the girls were in elementary school, and we decided we no longer needed or wanted live-in help. Instead, we hired Severina, a housekeeper and cook who worked for us during the week. She was ideal and stayed with us for about eight years. During that time, as the girls grew older, I reduced her household chores because Roy and I wanted our daughters to learn to be responsible for cleaning their rooms, washing dishes, and doing laundry.

How well I can relate to Michelle Obama's strict orders as First Lady when she instructed the White House staff not to make Malia's and Sasha's beds because she wants them to be responsible and self-reliant. Mrs. Obama and I have the same attitude about raising children: we don't think that it's right for children to grow up feeling entitled to have someone else take care of their needs.

*   *   *

I enjoyed working at Unified Services. In many ways it seemed as if I were running my own company, but without the burden of ownership. When people asked me if I had ever thought of starting my own business, my response was always "No, why would I?"

In fact, when one of Jerry's consultants was thinking of starting his own janitorial company, he asked me whether I would consider joining him, but I told him that I was perfectly content where I was. He wouldn't let up, however, and one day he put a different spin on his request. He started to enumerate what the benefits would be if I owned my own company. He went on and on about how he thought I should venture out on my own.

All along I kept saying to myself, *Why is he pushing so hard for me to start my company?* Then he threw down the gauntlet. He said, "Listen, Lillian, I thought I wanted to start my own company. I even filed my incorporation papers, but I decided to stick to consulting." He urged me to take the papers, change the name of the incorporators, and file the papers for myself. At first I didn't know what to say or how to react, but he had planted the seed. That's all it took.

I discussed the idea with Roy, who assumed the role of devil's advocate. He asked questions like "Why this business? Why not something in consulting?" In truth, I think he was hoping that

I would choose a more glamorous type of business than janitorial services. My response to him was, "This is the business that I know, and I think there's a lot of money to be made. Why go into something that I don't know?"

It seemed like a good time to start my own business, for I was vaguely aware that Congress was starting to talk about creating programs that would help businesses owned by women. Although I knew none of the details, I thought that if I could get a head start, I would be in a position to take advantage of whatever programs came along. I also knew from firsthand experience working in the janitorial industry that there were few female business owners and even fewer black female business owners—even though most of the workers were black women. After what seemed like endless discussions, Roy and I agreed that starting my own janitorial company was a good idea.

I filed my incorporation papers in December 1975. My plan was to continue working at Unified and build up my business on the side. This proved more difficult than I thought it would be. After working all day in the office and coming home to spend time with my family, I was too exhausted to think about my business venture. In addition, many things had to be conducted during normal business hours, and I did not have that flexibility. Consequently, I did little more than file the incorporation papers.

My "secret" business venture began weighing heavily on my mind. Although there were few people who knew about it, I was concerned that Jerry would find out. There was only one thing to do: I had to break the news to him myself. My nerves were on edge the day of our meeting. Jerry's initial reaction took me by surprise; he said that he was happy for me because he thought that I would do well going into business for myself.

Then he asked the question that I feared he would ask: "What kind of business are you going into?" I was quiet for a moment, then responded, "The janitorial business." He didn't say anything but the expression on his face spoke volumes of disappointment: his jaw dropped and a look of disbelief washed over his face.

I don't remember who broke the silence, but we ended the meeting agreeing that I would stay long enough for him to find and train my replacement. I thought the meeting ended cordially.

A few days later, a bomb fell. Jerry appeared at my office door and said, "Lincoln [which is how he referred to me], could I talk to you?" Hesitantly, I went into his office. That's when he told me that his board of directors had met and had decided that I should leave at the end of the week. I was taken aback, but I collected myself. The tension in the room was palpable. It was Wednesday, and it didn't make sense for me to stay the rest of the week. I left that afternoon with no job and no "real" company of my own yet.

I suddenly realized what had just happened: I had been fired. Centennial One, Inc., was founded that day.

CHAPTER

8

Life as a Double Minority Entrepreneur

Decide that you want it more than you are afraid of it.

—Bill Cosby

One day when I was shopping in a local store, I saw a woman smiling at me. It was when she approached me that I made the connection and remembered who she was.

"Hello, Mrs. Lincoln. How are you?" she said.

"I'm fine, and you?"

"You may not remember me, but I worked for you at Beltsville."

"Yes, I do remember you. Your first name is Josephine, but I can't remember your last name."

"It's Josephine Powell. I worked in building 301. I remember the first night you came out to interview us. You looked so nice. You were dressed in a pink suit, and you were so confident. You haven't changed. You look great."

"Thank you, Josephine."

That conversation with a former employee ten years after she had left Centennial One gave me a warm glowing feeling—to think that she remembered what I wore that night; I certainly didn't. She saw me as confident when in reality I had been nervous, not at all sure of how to approach a group of unhappy

153

employees who had just been laid off by their previous employer. There I was, on a job site at the Agricultural Research Center in Beltsville, Maryland, in a hot and overcrowded room, to conduct interviews for my first contract. In spite of all the experience I had at Unified Services, I had never been out in the field. Hiring was a job for operations managers. This was all new to me.

It was June 1976, and I felt as if I were about to parachute out of a plane, with my heart in my throat and my right hand clinging to the rip cord, praying that I would make a safe landing. Ever since I left the farm in 1958, I had been self-sufficient. Now, for the first time in my life, I had to rely on my husband's income— no small feat for the proud, independent woman I had become. It didn't help that we had grown accustomed to our dependable dual income, the luxury of live-in help, a home in the suburbs, two modern cars, and family vacations.

The climate for women in business at the time made matters a little more troubling. Female business owners constituted only a small percentage of business owners in the mid-1970s. Unlike today, there were few, if any, organizations or associations that supported women in their efforts to develop and grow their businesses. Even more daunting was that there were very few women in my industry. At all the national conventions and regional seminars that I had attended while I worked at Unified, I had met only one female owner. Ironically, janitorial services was an industry in which 90 percent of the hourly employees were women—minority women, at that—and the owners were typically white men. It would be twelve more years before Congress passed the Women's Ownership Act with the help of the National Association of Women Business Owners (NAWBO). The act was designed to provide the resources to help women develop their businesses. The bill was signed into law by President Reagan at a White House ceremony in 1988.

During this phase of my life, I also came to understand what it meant to stand up for myself as a double minority—that is, as both a woman and a black person. If the survival instinct in me hadn't made me as strong as steel, I could have easily succumbed to the setbacks and challenges of racial and sexual discrimination. However, I refused to give up the good fight. My motto, "Defeat is not an option," was my sword and shield, and it brought me to victory in my efforts to launch my business.

Nevertheless, my courage and determination didn't mitigate the reality I was up against. Like Sisyphus rolling the boulder up the mountain, I knew that starting my own company would be an uphill battle. I was charting unfamiliar (and rocky, in my case) territory. Unified proved to be a good training ground, but being an employee and owning a business are very different and require very different skills.

The only black business owners I knew operated small-scale neighborhood businesses, such as beauty salons, barbershops, or convenience stores (Aunt Alberta came to mind). However, I had higher aspirations and a grander vision: I envisioned that the world would be my marketplace. I recalled a piece of advice that Professor Fitzhugh had given his business students when he spoke of entrepreneurship as a state of mind: "You have to allow your mind to be exploratory." I interpreted his advice to mean that I had to be willing to take calculated risks and stay the course despite setbacks, challenges, and even failures. Above all, it meant that I couldn't be afraid of the unknown.

Thus, I took up the charge, wasting no time completing the incorporation papers to legalize the formation of my company and ensure that I was 100 percent owner. Roy and I had talked about owning the business together, but in the end he stated matter-of-factly that he didn't want to be a co-owner. I was just as happy to go it alone because I wasn't sure that mixing marriage and business was a good idea.

In truth, I think that Roy didn't want to have anything to do with the business because he questioned whether I would succeed, and he didn't want to be part of a losing venture. I also think, as I mentioned earlier, that he would have preferred that I start a business in a more prestigious industry—one that would have enhanced his social standing. With Roy, everything had to do with appearances and status, which was his downfall in the end.

His only commitment to my company was that he agreed to be a board member, but even that was short-lived. A few weeks after I incorporated, we were discussing a business issue—what it was I can't even recall—but I disagreed with him about a course of action that I thought we should take. He was so upset with me that he resigned from the board that very day. I readily accepted his letter of resignation, and I never invited him to join the board again.

*   *   *

Unified Services had provided a good foundation by exposing me to the workings of the Small Business Administration's (SBA) 8(a) program. Based on my dealings with the program, I knew that I was as good a candidate for the program as anyone—or so I thought. At that point, I had a narrow window of opportunity in which to apply to the 8(a) program; it was early June, and the government's fiscal year would end in less than four months.

My application to Harvard Business School was a walk in the park by comparison. For Harvard, I was required to write essays about myself and my experiences—situations that were right at my fingertips and of which I had an intimate understanding. This was not the case for the 8(a) program. This application required that I look into a crystal ball and glimpse the future. I had to write about the history of the company when the company wasn't more than a seed of an idea.

In short, the application was an exercise in writing fiction. Since I had no management team, I had to include résumés of managers who would theoretically make up my team. I had to provide detailed financial information, including five-year cash-flow projections, pro forma statements, and a summary of how the company would be capitalized (such as through bank loans and personal investments). In this regard, my HBS training came in handy because I was accustomed to manipulating and interpreting financial reports. The easiest part of the application was providing a list of current and potential customers, as well as references from people who could vouch for my professionalism and reputation.

I would learn many practical lessons as I developed my business over the next twenty-five years, but one valuable lesson that I learned right out of the gate was that your network is like a golden thread. If you respect it and treat it well, it will pay you back in kind.

Before I submitted my application to the 8(a) program, I thought it would be wise to better understand the application process to improve my chances of being accepted into the program. Going through my mental Rolodex of people who might be of help to me, I remembered a man whom I knew when I was at Unified Services. Wyn Smith, the director of SBA's Washington District Office. He was extremely knowledgeable about the 8(a) program, and I knew that he could give me some guidance and pointers about the application and acceptance process. My concern that he might not remember me was allayed as soon as I made the call. Not only did he take my call, he said he remembered me quite well. I don't know why I thought he wouldn't remember me, since there were so few women at the time who were in management positions.

Wyn responded positively when I told him of my plan to apply to the program, and he agreed to help me in any way he could—and he did. Going beyond the call of duty, he offered to shepherd my application through the system to ensure that it would get to the powers that be and, more important, that I would know within four to six weeks if my application had been accepted.

I felt like the luckiest person alive with Wyn on my side. In the meantime, he impressed upon me the importance of taking the initiative to personally market to the various government agencies, such as the Department of Defense and the Department of Commerce. In 1976, the process worked like this: federal agencies identified specific solicitations to be assigned to the 8(a) program. Serving as a broker, SBA would then designate a contractor to negotiate with the agency. Alternatively, the agency could request a specific contractor with whom it wanted to negotiate.

My strategy was to tap my network of contracting officers from my days at Unified Services and let them know that I was starting my own janitorial company. Whenever I placed a call to my contacts, I made sure to maintain accurate records of our conversations, noting their level of interest in working with me. These notes came in handy later, especially when I was required by SBA to provide evidence of my ability to secure contracts. I was ready at a moment's notice to produce the names of contracting officers who were eager to do business with me.

Developing good banking relationships was another principle that I would carry throughout my life because you never know when you're going to need a bank loan. After I submitted my application, it was time to secure a loan. I knew it would take some work to convince a banker to lend capital to a start-up, so it was important that I work with a banker who saw me as trustworthy. I knew just the banker: Bill Wilson, the newly elected president of a local bank. Having successfully worked with Bill when Roy and I needed to get personal loans, I was confident that he would see me as a person who would make good on my business loan. My strategy worked. I invited Bill to lunch at a moderately priced restaurant located near his office. I began the meeting with small talk to create a comfortable environment. Then I informed him of my plans to open my own business. He listened attentively as I proceeded to tell him that I would be making a personal investment in my business but that I also needed a bank loan. I wanted to impress upon him that I was a good risk because I was willing to invest some of my own money in the business. After all, why should the bank risk its assets if I wasn't willing to risk my own assets?

He promised to give my request consideration. A few days later he informed me that I had been approved for a $12,000 line of credit. This was short of a miracle, since most commercial lending is predicated on the pledge of a business's two primary assets, accounts receivables and inventory: I had neither. Without this line of credit, the chances that I would have been able to launch my company would have been slim.

My next step was to secure a supplier—a business from which I would purchase my cleaning supplies—and to convince it to give me a line of credit. This was another example of drawing on good relationships. I had established an amicable relationship with Milton Silverman, a top producer at American Supply Company, when the company was Unified's primary supplier. As Unified's controller, I always made sure that American Supply received most of our business and that we always paid our bills on time.

Since the lunch approach had worked so well with the banker, I decided to try it out with Milt, which is how I referred to him. He was not at all surprised when I told him that I was starting my own business. In fact, he was genuinely excited for me and promised to do everything he could to help me. Within days, he called to tell me that the company had agreed to give me a ninety-day line of credit—another miracle. In both cases, I'm sure that my Harvard MBA had something to do with assuring them that I was a savvy and smart businesswoman.

Armed with a line of credit from a bank and a supply company, I was now prepared to confront what would be my biggest and scariest cash outlay—payroll. To operate successfully in the janitorial industry, a company has to have adequate cash flow to meet payroll, which in most cases occurs on a weekly basis. The business model looks like a human pyramid, with the majority of workers—most of whom are unskilled, hourly wage earners—on the bottom and fewer, more skilled workers at the top. The job of an owner is to keep the pyramid working, and the only way to do this is to meet payroll.

At that point, I also realized that I couldn't continue working out of my home. I had already taken over the dining room and the living room. All the bedrooms were occupied. However, I knew that I needed to keep my overhead costs to a minimum, so I didn't want to sign a long-term lease. I hit upon the perfect solution: I decided to convert the garage into an office. This was an easy decision because the garage was used as storage space rather than to house our cars.

I was moving closer to having all the pieces in place for the opening of my company in October. It was mid-July, and I was busy marketing for prospective clients when SBA's national office lowered the boom: the program had rejected me. I couldn't understand why, so I called my reliable adviser, Wyn. He was just as perplexed as I was, but he assured me that he would look into the situation. He got back to me with a response that made no sense. The office told him that SBA could not guarantee that it could provide me with contracts.

My first thought was, *What are they talking about? I worked with this program for three years while I was employed at Unified. Not once do I remember SBA acquiring a contract for Unified.* I knew that Jerry had been responsible for securing his own. My next thought was, *This sounds a bit suspicious to me. Do I detect sex discrimination at play here?*

I responded to Wyn, "That's crazy! I don't expect, nor do I want, SBA to find contracts for me. I'm perfectly capable of finding my own." I then explained to Wyn my experience with Unified and how Jerry had aggressively marketed for new business. Wyn knew Jerry well and was aware of Jerry's masterful marketing efforts. Why would I expect to be treated differently? Wyn said he would look into the problem and get back to me. I was in a panic, knowing that the government's fiscal year would end in about two and a half months. Time was running out.

Just as he said he would, Wyn got back to me within a day. He told me that the national office would reconsider my application if I could provide them with evidence that I could get contracts. Provide them with evidence? What nerve! I wondered whether other applicants were required to do the same. This, however, was not the time to fight the double minority monster in the closet. Fortunately, I was prepared, and I provided SBA with a list of agencies and the names of contracting officers who would consider doing business with me. Two weeks later, I was accepted into the program.

I started to work with my target list when suddenly I struck gold. The contracting officer at Fort Belvoir, Virginia (whom I had met while working at Unified), told me that his contract with Unified was not being renewed. My antennae went up: I sensed that the relationship between Unified and Fort Belvoir had soured. This sounded like a perfect beginning and my lucky break.

I met with the officer to discuss the details of the contract. I assured him that I had the financing and management to take on the work. I almost fell over when he told me the size of the contract: $750,000—not bad for my first client! It was settled. The contracting officer said he would contact SBA and identify me as the company with which the agency wanted to negotiate the contract. I was on cloud nine.

It was now mid-August, and the contract was scheduled to begin October 1. I had a lot to do before the starting date. First on my list was to hire a number of employees and a secretary. However, once again I was stopped dead in my tracks. Only a week after my meeting with the Fort Belvoir officer, SBA called to inform me that I had been turned down for the contract.

No explanation was given. I had gotten used to being rejected by SBA, but this was ridiculous. I had done everything right and followed all the rules. My blood was boiling. I contacted SBA and warned the administration that I was prepared to take my case to my congressman if the agency obstructed my efforts to acquire contracts. I concluded: "I told you that I could find my own contracts, and I have done that, yet SBA has refused to designate me as the company to negotiate with Fort Belvoir. So I now expect SBA to assist me in finding another contract."

Although I didn't want to burn my bridges, I refused to be a pushover. I was prepared to fight for what I deserved, so I decided to move forward with my company plans, contract or no contract. (In this particular case, I suspect that the decision not to give me the Fort Belvoir contract was politically motivated. Since Unified Services had previously had the contract, SBA probably did not want to be put in the middle and give the impression that it had taken the contract from Unified and given it to a former Unified employee.)

In the first week in September, I received another call from SBA. My heart began to pound as I braced myself for more bad news.

SBA: "Hello. Mrs. Lincoln, please."

Me: "This is she."

SBA: "Mrs. Lincoln, I have good news. We have another opportunity for you to bid on a contract."

I nearly fainted. "Really?"

SBA: "Yes. The procurement is with the Agricultural Research Center in Beltsville, Maryland. The center has agreed to split one of its large contracts, retaining the current contractor for part of it and negotiating with Centennial for the other part."

Me: "That's great. How do I get started?" I thought, *Finally SBA has delivered.*

I kept my small victory to myself, not breathing a word to anyone for fear that I would be jinxed. My proposal was accepted, and I was awarded the contract. I now had to hire my workforce in time for the October 1 starting date.

The evening I walked into that large room to interview forty disgruntled people, who had just been laid off, for twenty positions was one of my scariest moments as a fledgling entrepreneur. I had no idea that this many people would show up, and I didn't have a clue about what to do. All I knew was that I had to think quickly on my feet. My HBS training came to the rescue: a Harvard MBA is like having a talisman in your back pocket that you secretly rub for good luck. I drew on the power of my degree, which I always wore undercover, to give me the confidence and authority to handle the crowd.

I told them about Centennial One, thanked them all for coming, explained the positions that were available, told them when the contract would begin, and asked them to complete their applications. I needed time to decide what hiring criteria I would use, so my stalling tactic was to say that my managers (there were none) would need time to review the applications, and we would notify everyone whether or not they were hired.

Trying to be fair in my evaluation of each candidate, I successfully hired a number of people, who remained with the company for many years. In formulating the hiring criteria, I thought about what characteristics would make for a good employee. For example, prior experience would be important. I know this sounds ironic coming from the young woman who once thought she didn't need practical experience to land a job, but it's different when you're sitting on the other side of the desk. Length of service would be another criterion; so would good references that stressed dependability, performance, attendance, and a good work ethic.

Centennial One was officially launched on October 1, 1976. After a year in business, I realized that SBA had done me a favor by not awarding me the $750,000 contract. It was much easier to deal with the problems of a $150,000 contract than of one five times as large.

I learned a great deal that first year about what it took to be an entrepreneur, including that luck, fate, timing, and tenacity had a hand in getting my business off the ground. In years to come, I would learn how to use my destiny as a trailblazing, barrier-breaking woman to inspire others to overcome hurdles and achieve their goals.

9

The Birth of a Company

*The determination to outwit one's situation means that
one has no models, only object lessons.*

—James Baldwin

In 2002, I received an invitation to speak in Boston at the annual conference of Harvard Business School's African American Student Union (AASU). Who would have thought that I would be standing in front of such a distinguished group of more than a hundred people—alumni, students, and prospective students? I had recently sold my business, after twenty-five years, and AASU wanted me to talk about my life as an entrepreneur. Taking questions from the audience was the most stimulating and the most revealing part of the evening.

A hand shot up from a young man in the audience. "Yes?" I asked, pointing my finger to acknowledge him.

"Mrs. Lambert, why would someone with a Harvard MBA choose to go into the janitorial business instead of a more sophisticated profession?"

I thought, *I give this young man credit for raising a question that a lot of people in this room are probably dying to ask but wouldn't dare, for fear of sounding disrespectful, or worse, hurting my feelings.*

"I'm glad you asked," I replied. "I'll be the first to admit that there's nothing sexy or glamorous about my industry. And you're right, it's not an industry in which you find many, if any, MBAs, much less a Harvard MBA. But I'll let you in on a secret: owning the mop is a lot different from pushing the mop."

A hush fell over the room: heads nodded as if to say, "Touché." I then explained that the one thing I had learned about business as a Harvard student poring over complex case studies was that regardless of the industry, business is business, and there's nothing glamorous about preparing budgets, making financial projections, and raising capital.

My decision to start a janitorial company was based on two motivations. First, I knew that I had a greater chance of succeeding in an industry in which I had prior practical experience, a good reputation, good working relationships, and a proven track record. Second, I felt more useful working in the janitorial business than I did working for social justice in the nonprofit sector. In fact, when I thought back to my two previous jobs working at the National Bankers Association and Sterling Institute, it depressed me, because both organizations ran out of money before they accomplished their goals.

Through my own experience, I learned that social purpose is sometimes found in the most unlikely places—the janitorial business, for instance. Who would have ever thought that the janitorial industry would give me a chance to have a positive effect on the lives of minorities (mostly blacks and Hispanics)? At the height of my company, I had more than twelve hundred employees. No social service job would have allowed me to improve the socioeconomic status of disadvantaged people on the scale that my company allowed me to do.

From the minute I launched Centennial One, I was determined to make it a different kind of cleaning service— one that held itself to high moral standards and treated its employees with dignity and fairness. The industry had a reputation for its owners mistreating its employees and lining their own pockets. I wanted to show those egotistical men (and they *were* all men) who lived high on plastic, drove fancy European cars, built McMansions, and rewarded themselves to the detriment of their employees what it's like to have a woman in the industry.

* * *

Having landed my first contract with the Agricultural Research Center, I was now in a financial position to spring into action and hire my first employee. Maxine Nicholas was hired to answer the phone and manage the administrative details that came with the contract. She had worked with me at Unified but had left, right before I did, for another position.

When I told her that I was also leaving Unified to start my own company, she had expressed an interest in working for me. Although I could not afford to hire her immediately, I promised that I would contact her as soon as I was in a position to do so. I was still operating out of my garage when I called Maxine, but her presence legitimized my company as a professional outfit. Before she came on board, I was it—the receptionist, the salesperson, the marketing person, and, of course, the controller.

Through Maxine I learned an important principle that became the bedrock of my company: if I can help to improve just one person's life, I have accomplished my goal. Watching Maxine grow into her administrative role was like watching a caterpillar transform into a monarch butterfly. There seemed to be no end to what Maxine was able and willing to do. I trained her to be the bookkeeper, and in no time she was preparing payroll and the company's monthly financial statements.

I would often think, *Here's a bright young lady with potentially a good future, but she needs a college degree.* As soon as this thought became lodged in my brain, I found myself sounding like my good old cousin Rudy when he kept nagging me about going to college. However, Maxine was not kin, so I had to be careful not to impose my views on her. Instead, I stressed the importance of education in a general way.

It must have worked. One day, to my delight, Maxine announced that she was enrolling in night school at the local community college. I saw a pattern: I had gone to night school while holding down a job. Then, after a year of attending night school, she announced that she was planning to move back to Virginia to enroll in a full-time college program. The pattern continued: she was again following in my footsteps.

It was bittersweet to let Maxine go after three years, but I knew that she was making the right decision. It was also payback time, and I wanted to show her my support in the same way that Ruth DiMisa, my boss at the Peace Corps, had supported me when I was a student at Howard: she had fought with the higher-ups to retain me as a part-time employee—something the administration had been reluctant to do.

Thus, it seemed only right for me to tell Maxine that a job would be waiting for her if or when she returned to Maryland. For the next three summers, Maxine came back to work for me. Years later, when we bumped into each other at a professional organization, she told me that I was her role model who inspired her to continue her education. I was touched to know that I had a positive influence on her life. I'm also glad that the accounting skills she learned under my watch paid off. Today Maxine enjoys her job as a business manager for the city of Hopewell, Virginia.

There is a perennial academic debate about whether leadership is an inborn or a learned trait. Based on my personal experience, I'd say it's both. For a person to be a leader, he or she must first have an innate and genuine interest in motivating people. For example, there are some people who would never take a leadership position for all the money in the world. Instead, they prefer to be a cog in a wheel, performing a specific function.

Having a genuine interest in people, however, is not enough to be a good leader. I believe that leaders learn how to lead through practical experience and on-the-job training. No advanced degree (even a Harvard MBA) or books on leadership could have made me a leader. I had to learn by working in the trenches and interacting with people every day; only then did I acquire effective leadership skills.

While I was busy developing Maxine's administrative skills, she was busy grooming me to become a compassionate leader. Maxine made me understand how important it is for a leader to respect and nourish the spirit of the whole person. In an industry in which the workforce comprises people who perform menial jobs, it is absolutely essential for an individual in my position to understand the personal burdens that beset blue-collar workers.

Very early in my career at Centennial, I created the principle "the whole person comes to work." In other words, I believe that if an employee has a personal problem, he or she does not check it at the door; the problem follows the person to work. This was the case with Maxine, who breathed a sigh of relief when I told her that she could bring her daughter to work. As a working mother of two young girls, I knew all too well what it was like to have to worry about day care while earning a living. As Maxine and I got to know each other better, I even encouraged her to join my church. Not only did she join the church, she also joined me in the choir, where we both sang alto.

As I set out to build my workforce, I clung to my credo of helping to improve people's lives. I went out of my way to hire people who on the surface didn't look like they had much going for them, but, who upon closer examination showed promise. In some cases, I was even willing to hire what the industry considered a "thorny population"—undesirable and therefore unemployable—in the hope that I could help turn their lives around.

The cards were stacked against most of them, but that didn't stop me from trying to give them a chance in life. Some had criminal records for misdemeanors such as underage drinking or possession of alcohol or marijuana. Since my clients required janitorial contractors (which is what I was) to secure police records of employees who were going to be assigned to their facilities, it was impossible for me to conceal this information. It broke my heart when I learned that I couldn't hire a person whom I thought worthy because of a record for what seemed like a minor offense. I wonder whether my clients used the same screening criteria when they hired their own people. I doubt it.

I hired at least a dozen young college-bound students who were looking for summer jobs. After a summer of janitorial work, many of them readily admitted to me that they were inspired to take their academic studies more seriously and complete their education. I took their evaluation as a compliment. If I had helped them set their sights high, then I had done a good thing.

*   *   *

At the end of my first year with the Agricultural Research Center contract, I posted a profit of $12,000 on sales of $212,000. This was a good omen, since most small businesses lose money the first year; some businesses even wallow in red ink for years after they open their doors. This particular contract served me well for eleven years, growing to more than $1 million by the time I graduated from the 8(a) program.

In my second year, 1978, I won a major contract with the Naval Research Center for nearly $500,000, but not without a hard fight. The contract came my way because I heeded the advice of a contracting officer at the Department of Navy who had told me to stay in touch with him because "you never know when something may become available."

Acting on his advice, every month or so I made a point of calling him, just to check in. However, on one particular day, he surprised me with a call to tell me that the navy had a job that might be of interest to me. He asked me to come to his office to pick up a procurement package. I could hardly contain myself: I was jumping up and down in my garage-turned-office as I hung up the phone, shouting, "Oh, my God, I can't believe it!" Fortunately, no one was at home to hear me carrying on like a crazy lady. If I had a bottle of champagne, I would have popped the cork that very second and drunk the whole bottle by myself to celebrate. Although I did not know the dollar amount of the contract, I knew enough about the size of the navy facilities to know that they were talking about very large buildings that came with a hefty price tag.

The procurement package was as heavy as a brick, containing page after page of specific requirements and complex instructions on how to prepare the proposal. Anyone who is familiar with government procurements knows the mind-boggling, "cross every *T,* dot every *I,*" time-consuming detail that goes into responding to a request for a proposal. That said, I wasn't flustered, because I already knew how to put a proposal together from having bid on the Agricultural Research Center contract. Thank God for small favors.

With the help of an outside consultant, I went straight to work writing narratives that outlined the work schedule of my employees, and I came up with price estimates for the various buildings based on the square footage. The proposal was exceptionally challenging to complete because the dozen or so buildings were scattered on two campuses that were fifty miles apart. In effect, I had to prepare two separate proposals: one for the research center in Annapolis, Maryland, and the other for the facility in Bethesda, Maryland. Each complex would require its own cleaning staff and means of transportation.

I remember all too well the day I was called in to negotiate the contract. There were four of us sequestered in a room: three navy civilian employees (two men and a woman) and me. The head negotiator appeared at first to be a kind, easygoing, cooperative guy, but my impression of him changed throughout the course of the day. The second man was quiet and didn't add much to the discussion. The woman, Shirley Jones, is imprinted on my brain for life.

I believe that every person we meet, for better or worse, comes into our lives to teach us a lesson. It's up to us to look at every encounter and ask ourselves, "What can I learn from this person?" It wasn't long before I realized why Mrs. Jones came into my life and what lesson I had to learn. She was a middle-aged woman who spoke firmly and was a stickler for detail.

As the key administrator, Mrs. Jones was the main point of contact with the winning contractor. On that particular negotiating day, she did nothing to make me feel comfortable about the possibility of our developing a good working relationship if I were to get the job. Mrs. Jones was in the seat of power; if she was unhappy, everyone was unhappy.

Nearly three hours into a meeting that seemed to be going nowhere, it became clear that the negotiation process had stalled. The lead negotiator took this as a sign that we needed to take a break. I was thankful for the relief: our faces had hardened into glowering stares, as if rigor mortis had set in.

As the top negotiator and I walked out of the room together, he started to "chat me up." I was caught a little off guard because his demeanor seemed to have softened, but only for a split second. The conversation suddenly turned to my family, and he asked me if I had any children. I answered, "Why, yes, I have two girls, four and six." His back stiffened like a porcupine, and he shot back at me, "I think they are too young for you to be out working."

There I was, trying to land a half-million-dollar contract with a man who was implying that I was shirking my responsibility as a mother. Today this attitude is anachronistic, and such a comment could even result in a lawsuit, but at that time this man sincerely believed that women with young children should be full-time homemakers. In fact, I'd venture to say that he exemplified the attitudes of most men in that era. In the 1970s, men didn't feel comfortable working with women in high positions, which made work for me as a black woman even more challenging. Nevertheless, I was the double minority that wouldn't go away, and I don't suffer fools gladly. His insult made me more determined than ever to win the contract.

I looked him straight in the eye and calmly assured him that my children were loved and well taken care of by their father and me. That was the end of our discussion. When we returned to the office, I methodically and tenaciously negotiated one of the toughest and most rewarding contracts of my career.

Over the years, I even came to appreciate Mrs. Jones, who enforced the contract to the letter. For example, if the agreement stated that the floors were to be stripped quarterly, it made no difference to her if they still retained a brilliant sheen at the time a stripping was scheduled. She insisted that they be redone in accordance with the schedule. Stripping the floors meant ruining the luster that my employees had worked so hard to obtain. Such unnecessary work would often upset my employees and give me pause as well. Couldn't she see that the floors were gleaming? In the end, however, Mrs. Jones's by-the-book, nitpicking demands better prepared me to handle any hard-nosed contract administrator who came my way. If I could handle Mrs. Jones, I could handle anyone. That was the lesson she taught me.

My revenues in the second year continued to increase, and in the third year Centennial went through such a growth spurt that the time had come for me to move out of my garage into a real office. I found a thousand-square-foot rental in a small office building about five miles from home, in Crofton, Maryland. The space—three offices and a reception area—was just the right size for building a professional staff, beginning with two vital functions: operations and human resources.

Starting a company is like having a baby. You give birth to your creation and then you have the responsibility to raise it. I took my responsibility one step further: Centennial was my baby, and all the people in it were my children, as well. I was determined to create a nourishing, familylike environment in which everyone could grow and thrive.

Even though I was the owner, I wanted to make my employees feel comfortable talking to the boss, so I employed a subtle technique: I'd leave my office door open, and when an employee walked by, I'd wave and say something like, "Hi, how are you today? How's your family?" This small gesture was enough to make my employees see that I was approachable and welcoming. Invariably, passersby would stop and come into my office to chat, even if just for a moment. In this regard, I made a concerted effort to learn the names of most of my employees as well as the names of their spouses and children.

The next phase was without a doubt the single most critical aspect of building my company. Because I believe that a leader is only as good as the people he or she leads, my philosophy was to hire bright, ambitious people and give them the freedom and authority to use their talents and skills to accomplish the company's goals. To this end, I spotted two young men who fit the bill. Over the next two decades, these two men would rise to high-level positions, using their natural talents and acquired skills and knowledge to help me build a successful company. One man remained loyal to me to the end; the other eventually rebelled against me. The latter situation was another lesson in leadership: a leader must never let down her guard but must remain vigilant of those who garner (too much) power.

I'll begin with my loyal employee, Legusta Floyd. As a human resource professional, Legusta did more than espouse my values: he gave the human resource function a whole new dimension. As challenging as it was to be innovative and creative in an industry that had the reputation for being backward and unimaginative, Legusta, whom I dubbed my whiz kid, defied the odds and introduced forward-thinking initiatives to create a family-oriented, respectful work environment.

A less talented and less competent person would have been daunted by the challenges that lay before him. He certainly had his work cut out for him. I never did like the word *janitor,* for instance: I thought it had a demeaning connotation. I challenged him to come up with a new title for hourly employees who cleaned the buildings. He did, and soon they were called *maintenance specialists.*

Legusta also took up my whole-person-comes-to-work philosophy. He adopted a state program called the Employee Assistance Program and made it available to all the employees in the company, regardless of rank. The service provided confidential counseling to troubled employees and their families. Although it was hard to quantify the success of this initiative, because of the confidential nature of the services, we noticed a marked improvement in many employees' performance and attendance over the years.

One of the employee initiatives that I'm most proud of was the Corporate College Program, which was the brainchild of Legusta and the other young man, the one who eventually became my second in command. This was Centennial's own degree program, designed to provide all employees, including the executive staff, with an advancement track of their own choosing. For example, if a maintenance specialist showed an interest in a particular position—such as learning how to operate a buffing machine—and was willing to put in the time to be trained, he or she would be put on an advancement track after all the requirements of that position had been met.

I remember one particular employee, Cesar, who was hired as a maintenance specialist. After attending many training programs, he was fast-tracked, receiving promotion after promotion, from working supervisor to managing supervisor to area manager. At one point, he proudly told me that his goal was to someday become president of Centennial. I told him, "That's my kind of spirit."

In an industry known for high employee turnover and on-site accidents, we were determined to be the exception to the rule. What was required was thinking outside the box, which Legusta was capable of doing. He never ceased to amaze me: you could present him with a systemic problem, and he would find the cure.

The Safety Bingo Game, with a cash reward, was an example. Legusta heard about this program, which was being used in another company, and he introduced the game to Centennial in an effort to promote a safe work environment and decrease employee turnover. The rule was that only employees who had completed the sixty-day safety probationary period and had perfect attendance were eligible to play.

The game became so popular that it was necessary to allow for multiple winners, with prizes ranging from twenty-five to a hundred dollars. The ultimate benefit of Safety Bingo was that it reduced the number of workers' compensation claims, which in the janitorial business can skyrocket out of control. A less obvious benefit, but perhaps more important in the long run, was that it improved attendance and enhanced teamwork: if a job site had a safety violation, the entire site was automatically eliminated from the game that day. In addition, an absent employee was not eligible to participate, even if the winning number appeared on his or her card.

Centennial also published a company newsletter, *Centennial Star,* that served as the employees' voice. There's nothing unusual about company newsletters, but we wanted to distinguish ours by making it employee-centered, so we published information that pertained specifically to employees instead of the company. My employees were always eager to share information with their colleagues about important milestones in their lives: births, engagements, weddings, and college-bound children.

One of the most memorable events in the company's history took place in 1998, when the company organized a trip to Disney World in Orlando, Florida, for about forty employees who were celebrating long-term anniversaries with the company. Depending on the employee's number of years of service, the company paid all or a portion of the expenses. I was glad to be part of a celebration in which rank and titles did not exist. It was like one big happy family: we went on rides together and ate together. A real treat was that the employees had a chance to meet and socialize with the family members of their coworkers.

*   *   *

While I was building my company's infrastructure, I was also establishing my reputation as an industry leader—and as a black female pioneer. However, my double minority status came with a heavy weight. In the mid-1970s, the prevailing attitude was that women in leadership roles had to be twice as good as their male counterparts in order to be considered half as good. As a black female leader, I had the additional burden of having to be twice as good as white women, too.

Nevertheless, as one who had grown accustomed to being the lone black woman in a white male–dominated industry, I wasn't fazed in the least by this challenge. By joining the Building Service Contractors Association International when I was employed at Unified Services, I had already raised my visibility in the organization by chairing committees, conducting workshops, speaking at conventions, and writing articles for the association's magazine. Thus, in time, I had gained a reputation as a doer and had earned the respect of my colleagues. The culmination of my efforts was to be elected president of this two-thousand-member international association in 1995, becoming the first woman to serve in that position. During my tenure, the organization had one of its most profitable years.

Assuming a leadership role in my industry resulted in my being recognized by my peers and winning many awards, which in turn put me in a good position to win new contracts, especially as I expanded my business into the private sector. One award that was a publicity windfall was the Small Business Person of the Year for the State of Maryland. I was given this award in 1981, when I had been in business for four years. I received many letters of congratulations, articles were written about me, and I was a guest of honor at a state-sponsored luncheon hosted by the lieutenant governor of Maryland.

The award activities culminated with a reception in the Rose Garden at the White House. I didn't meet any high-level officials in President Reagan's administration, but it didn't matter. It was an honor simply to be there. More than the award itself, however, what touched my heart was learning that Jerry Davis, my former boss at Unified Services, was the one who had nominated me for the award. This magnanimous gesture showed Jerry's true character. He was an outstanding human being who had decided that it was beneath him to hold a grudge.

*   *   *

Just as my company was gaining traction and becoming profitable—revenues had grown to $3 million annually, with three hundred employees—I was beginning to feel an undertow at home. My relationship with Roy was as much a mystery to me as it must have been to anyone who knew us. To think that a tough-minded businesswoman who could turn a bully into a coward in a professional situation would then succumb to the pressures, whims, and wishes of her husband is puzzling, if not disturbing. I was the woman who had struck the word *obey* from her wedding vows, yet my relationship with my husband fit the old advertising jingle, "She can bring home the bacon, fry it up in a pan, and never let him forget he's a man."

My marriage began to decline when Roy saw the financial rewards of my company as a good reason to buy a bigger home in a better neighborhood, and it ended when I violated my own rule about mixing marriage and business by bringing Roy into the business.

Before we made our ill-fated move to a new home in 1981, everything had been going our way. Roy was doing well in his job as an accountant with the National Labor Relations Board; my mother was actively involved in senior citizens' activities at the local community center; and the girls were well adjusted and excelling in our neighborhood's public school—which laid to rest, at least for the time being, the public-versus-private-school debate that Roy and I had been having about what kind of education we wanted for the girls.

Two years after we settled into our new home in Davidsonville, I saw an excellent opportunity to expand the business by acquiring a local janitorial supply company located in Springfield, Virginia, just outside Washington, D.C. I bought all the assets of the company, including the name. This was a natural acquisition: Centennial was purchasing thousands of dollars' worth of supplies and equipment on a monthly basis, so why shouldn't we reap the benefits of owning such a company? Furthermore, since the new acquisition would exist as a separate company, it would be positioned to offer supplies not only to Centennial but to other companies as well. The new company provided another revenue stream. However, as I would soon learn, expanding a company comes with a price: it presents a whole new set of issues that an owner must be able to handle.

Shortly after acquiring this new company, I started to think about adding a full-time finance professional to my executive staff. Up to that point I was the one who oversaw the finance function, but I was tiring of the position and finding it a bit taxing. Perhaps I was having a midcareer crisis, but I was feeling restless and in need of a new challenge that would get me away from working behind a desk, crunching numbers. From my involvement in the industry's association and other public relations appearances, I realized that I enjoyed serving as the public face of the company, and I wanted to become more involved in industry events.

Thoughts about looking for my replacement must have been weighing heavily on my mind, because in a moment of weakness (I don't know what possessed me), I jokingly turned to Roy and said to him, "Maybe you should join the company and be the controller." Without giving it a second thought, Roy responded, "That's a great idea. I think I will."

My heart sank with the force of the *Titanic* hitting the ocean floor. I wasn't at all serious. In fact, I was stunned that he would even think of giving up his secure government job. Moreover, even though Roy was an accountant, I didn't think he was a good money manager based on how he handled his personal finances. His spending habits were so out of control that we had agreed that I would handle the family finances.

If I could have retracted any offer in my life, it would have been this. Unfortunately, he was my husband, and I had to live with the consequences. As much as I was horrified by what I had just done, I tried to rationalize my decision, thinking that at least the money would stay in the family. Besides, I would still be there to oversee the finance function and prevent a catastrophe from happening.

For the next few months, it actually looked as though my decision to hire Roy had turned out to be a wise one. His presence in the office at least made it possible for me to steal away for a couple of hours to tend to personal matters, usually ones that concerned our girls' school activities or doctors' appointments. However, no sooner had I come full circle in my thinking than I started to notice that procedures were breaking down in the finance department. Financial statements were being produced later and later in the month. When I asked to see the bank reconciliation statements, Roy couldn't furnish any. Things were going from bad to worse. He was not paying vendors on time, nor was he collecting receivables on time. To compensate for the cash-flow shortage, he drew on the company's line of credit. This was too much for me to bear, and I finally confronted him.

Just as I had begun to notice in our marriage, he always had a seemingly justifiable reason for why things were not done right, coupled with a promise that it wouldn't happen again. After a few stiff conversations, we both agreed that things weren't working out in the office. To lessen the blow of firing him outright, I weaned him from the position over a one-year period and changed his position to that of an outside consultant.

This put a greater strain on me because I now had to take back much of the finance job, which was something I had wanted to relinquish. This was a frustrating situation for both of us, but

I've always been amazed by how well Roy handled it. Most men would have been crushed to have been fired by their wives, but Roy didn't let this incident rob him of his pride and self-image. I don't know how he did it, but he was always able to maintain an appearance of happiness and well-being.

Roy did not let this latest incident keep him from launching his own financial management firm, which, in my opinion, was perhaps the worst decision he could have made. I thought he needed a job in which he would be supervised, but I kept my thoughts to myself. Nonetheless, the writing was on the wall. Although he got his business off the ground, it never took off. It became more of a hobby than a business, even though he had a few employees.

The final act was when we received a letter of notification from the state of Maryland that a lien had been placed on our home. Apparently, Roy had not paid the withholding taxes for his business. When I approached him with the letter, he assured me that it was a mistake and that he would take care of it. Of course I didn't believe that he would, but I didn't want to argue with him.

Instead, I conducted my own investigation. I talked to the office that issued the letter to find out what the lien meant. Having dealt with the IRS when I was at Unified Services, I knew the gravity of the situation. The future of my business and home were at stake. I couldn't believe that Roy had the gall to put his family in such financial peril.

By this time, I had lost all respect for Roy as a man and a husband. I had to face something that I had been trying to avoid for a long time. My siblings had gone through divorces, and I had always said that I did not want that to happen to me. I held out for as long as I could, hoping and praying for a miracle, but I knew I was heading for a divorce.

Money issues are often cited as the number one reason that marriages fail, and I certainly believe that this was the primary cause of the failure of my marriage. In our case, it had nothing to do with our not having enough money. We were very comfortable and did not want for anything. The problem was our differing attitude toward money. It didn't matter that Roy and I came from the same socioeconomic bracket; he was always reaching for a more ostentatious lifestyle. He thought nothing of writing bad checks to buy things like jewelry, cars, or high-fashion clothes that we could not afford. I, on the other hand, was disciplined and frugal. Saving for a rainy day had been ingrained in me since childhood.

Although Roy did not want a divorce, he knew that I was at my wits' end, and we agreed to part ways. The girls and I remained in the house. He found a town house not far from us to make it easy for him to see Darnetha and Tasha.

Roy's pride was both a blessing and a curse. He didn't lay any claim to my business—even though, according to my attorney, he was entitled as my husband to half of the business because it had been built during our marriage. Roy also offered to pay an amount of child support that I knew he could not afford. He insisted, however, and for the next two years, I sporadically received child support payments. I didn't pursue the unpaid amount, remembering instead his kindness in not cashing in on my business. The girls, Mom, and I did not suffer, because I was confident that I could maintain a comfortable standard of living. I also wanted to make sure that the girls' relationship with their father, whom they adored, remained positive. I made a promise to myself never to say anything negative to them about their dad.

I agonized over when would be a good time and place to break the news of my pending divorce to my family, only to discover that there was no opportune time. What I did discover, however, was that the people we live with are more perceptive than we give them credit for being. Although I thought I was letting out a big, dark secret, not one family member was surprised. It demonstrated to me just how much we reveal about ourselves and our emotional states even when we try to disguise them. Roy and I had never talked about our relationship around the girls or Mom, yet our body language and the way we related to each other must have spoken volumes.

I was taken aback by Darnetha's response when she said, "I knew you guys were not getting along. I know you both still love us, but you can't stay married—that's not a surprise." Years later when she reached adulthood, she confessed that it wasn't until her dad actually moved out that the ramifications of our divorce hit her, and she felt very sad for her father.

Our divorce had a more negative effect on Tasha. I would occasionally overhear her telephone conversations with her father, and she would ask if he was okay and if he was taking his medicine. (Roy died from diabetes-related complications in 1996.) I felt a tug on my heart when I heard the tenderness in Tasha's voice; yet I'd wonder why she didn't seem to show the same concern for me. I later realized that this was a selfish thought, because she was a young child who felt the loss of an important person in her life. Roy would always refer to Darnetha and Tasha as "my girls." They felt the same way: they were his girls. Just as parents love their children in different ways, children have the same right to express their love for their parents in the way that best suits their personalities.

My mother's response to my divorce was the most shocking of all. She was in Ballsville visiting a friend when Roy and I made the decision to end our marriage. My concern about telling my mother was heightened by the fact that she had been married to my father for forty years before he died, and I knew that she had endured the ups and downs of a marriage and had made many sacrifices. Now I was throwing in the towel after seventeen years.

As I usually did on her visits to Ballsville, I drove down to pick her up, stopping first in Richmond for my brother Willie John, who would accompany me for the rest of the trip. We considered it to be a family reunion on wheels. On the way to Richmond from Maryland, I practiced various ways to break the news to Mother, but the words eluded me. As soon as I picked up Willie John, I told him about Roy and me. He wished me luck, but he had no advice on how to tell Mother. So much for his help.

It seemed like an eternity before we finally arrived in Ballsville to pick up Mother. On the return trip home to Maryland, I was becoming crazily nervous, wondering how she was going to react to the news. I expected her to lecture me, telling me that I needed to hang in there and work it out. Mother was sitting in the backseat; Willie John was in the front seat. All of a sudden, the words just flew out of my mouth: "Mom, when you get back to Maryland, you will no longer have a son-in-law at the house. We've decided to get a divorce."

Without missing a beat, she responded: "I wondered what took you so long." I was flabbergasted. Was this Mama speaking? I glanced at Willie John, who had a look of shock on his face. Even though Mom's response was unexpected, I was relieved that I did not get the lecture that I was sure would come. The rest of the ride home was less tense as we talked about other things to lighten the atmosphere.

After my separation and ultimate divorce, I was left with an uncertain future. I was living in the country on two acres of land in a thirty-five-hundred-square-foot house with my mother and two adolescent daughters, who all depended on me more than ever. There was the additional burden of mowing the lawn and maintaining the swimming pool. These were once Roy's responsibilities. Now they were mine.

10

Letting Go and Moving On

Never work just for money or for power. They won't save your soul or build a decent family or help you sleep at night.

—Marian Wright Edelman

It's been said that God never gives us a challenge that we don't have the strength to bear. In that regard, God gave me 1985. Not only did my marriage unravel, but my business also started spinning out of control. Just two weeks after Roy and I decided to separate, the Small Business Administration notified me that I was "graduating" from the 8(a) program, effective immediately. This was SBA's way of saying that I would be expelled from the program. The notification was a huge blow. At the time, Centennial, now in its ninth year, had yearly revenues of approximately $7.5 million, with about $5 million attributed to 8(a) contracts. I was now facing the loss of two-thirds of my business over the next six months.

Although I had begun to lay the groundwork to prepare for the day that I would no longer qualify to participate in the program, I had much work to do to ensure that my business wouldn't be negatively affected. Because I had anticipated that I could be expelled after nine years, I had acted on the advice of some colleagues and had submitted a request the year before to SBA for a one-year extension. I was hoping to use the extension as a grace period to fortify my company's position in the marketplace. SBA, however, took one year to respond to my request, and its response was a letter notifying me that I was no longer in the program. Just like that, I was ejected—a setback that nearly rocked the foundation of my company.

Saddled with capital and overhead expenses—I had nearly five hundred employees and had just signed a long-term lease on office space—my company posted its first loss in its history after the first year out of the program. The situation was grim, but I acted on a mantra that has never failed me in the face of overwhelming obstacles: *Cancel your pity party and do something proactive.*

Taking draconian, cost-cutting measures to prevent my company from bleeding to death, I cut my salary and froze the salaries of key executives, managers, and administrative staff. No one was happy, but everyone understood that bold action had to be taken to keep the company afloat. I must have done something right because my employees stood by my side, remaining loyal and steadfast in their efforts to do everything they could to help us get through tough times.

In particular, my operations manager, LeRoy Dock, who had become my right-hand man at this point, and his staff played key roles in working with me through this difficult transition. Under his supervision, all contracts were reevaluated to see where we could cut operating costs without compromising service. He also worked very closely with Legusta, my human resources professional, to find creative ways to retain and keep our hourly employees motivated. (At this stage in his career, LeRoy was a gem who demonstrated extraordinary leadership, management, and negotiation skills. This would change over time.)

I had something else working in my favor. I had wisely heeded the counsel of Professor Fitzhugh, who had repeatedly emphasized a fundamental principle of running a successful business: "Plow your profits back into your company to build up cash reserves for unexpected downturns." As soon as Centennial had begun turning a profit, I made sure that a healthy portion of the profits went back into the company's retained earnings. This cash reserve is what got us through the lean years.

The crisis also had a silver lining. Knowing that one day I would need to replace the federal contracts that I was obtaining through the 8(a) program, I had hired a director of marketing to expand our efforts into the private sector. Even though I had majored in marketing as an undergraduate, it was not my area of interest. Finance became my passion.

Another business principle that I had absorbed as an undergraduate and that served me well when I hired my marketing director was this: "Surround yourself with people who complement your skills, not those who duplicate them." Even though only a few contracts materialized in the first eighteen months of his tenure, my marketing director turned out to be one of the best investments I ever made in the company. In time, he began to attract a new type of clientele from private industries, and we began winning contracts from blue-chip companies like ABC News, Procter & Gamble, Westinghouse, Baltimore Gas & Electric, Potomac Electric, Fannie Mae, and Computer Science. (Most if not all of these contracts were secured through the company's membership in the MD/DC Supplier Development Council, an organization composed of minority-owned firms and major corporations whose mission is to do business with one another.)

That was the good news. The not-so-good news was that the profit margin for private-sector contracts did not compare to those for the 8(a) contracts. Industry research had shown that gross profits on government contracts ranged from 12 to 18 percent, with net profits ranging from 5 to 10 percent. Private contract profit margins were one-third to one-half the margin of government contracts. The bottom line was that the revenues from private-sector contracts had to be two to three times the revenues from government contracts just for the company to stay even.

I was astute enough to realize that I could not turn the company around solely by cutting costs and depending on the private contracts that we had won. I had to be willing to pull out all the stops and implement some aggressive growth strategies, knowing full well that every decision I made and every action I took would be a do-or-die scenario. Expanding into new markets, while risky, was my best chance of saving the company.

I thought back to orientation at Harvard Business School when Dean Baker had uttered these words to the incoming class: "[The case method of study] may be the only time in your life when you can make a decision and not have to live with it." At the time, I didn't digest the full meaning of this statement, but now I understood it. As a businesswoman faced with the enormous task of saving my business, I had to accept the consequences of my decisions, which I prefer to call taking calculated risks.

Richmond, Virginia, seemed like an ideal location to open an office for two reasons. First, it was a sizable metropolitan area. Second, it was just a hundred miles from our main office in Maryland, which meant that I could keep an eye on it. To drum up business in the area, I began attending some business opportunity affairs sponsored by the Virginia Minority Supplier Development Council.

That's when I met Daisy Williams, the director of the Minority Business Enterprise Office for the state of Virginia. She was more than an ally; she was heaven-sent. Not only did she encourage me to market to the state agencies, she also wasted no time in scheduling appointments for me to meet with key procurement officers. She crammed as many meetings as possible into one day because she knew that I was traveling from Maryland and wanted to make the trip worth my while.

The first two meetings were disastrous. The procurement officers showed little or no interest in my marketing presentation. As I headed off to lunch, I was overcome with dread as I thought about my two afternoon appointments. Then something awful happened that confirmed one of my worst fears. I got a call informing me that my one o'clock meeting had been canceled.

My initial thought was, *Great! I may as well cancel my other meeting and head back to Maryland to beat rush-hour traffic. I'm wasting my time in Richmond. It's obvious that there's no interest in my company here.*

As I was about to pick up the phone to cancel the next appointment, I was thrown off by what seemed to be an inner voice saying, *Don't do it.* This was as close as I would ever come to having an out-of-body experience, but at that moment, I felt a strange hand come out of thin air, take the phone from me, and put it back on the receiver. I waited in quiet despair for two hours until my next meeting.

There were two elderly white men waiting to hear my sales pitch for the state of Virginia contract. Much to my surprise, they were warm and welcoming, which was the opposite of how I had been received earlier in the day. As I gave my presentation, I could tell that they were listening until I finished. The senior gentleman broke the silence and said, "Mrs. Lincoln, we've heard all of this before. Why should we believe you over all the other contractors who have been here before you?" Never had I heard such blunt, plainspoken English. I don't know where the words came from, and I honestly don't even remember what I said, but whatever it was, I must have alleviated their concerns.

The gentleman's response to my defense was positive. He asked me to prepare a proposal for two buildings that were currently under contract. Although he didn't reveal the budget, he did say enough to make me understand that they were not at all happy with the performance of the existing contractor. That was all I needed for me to feel confident that I was a serious contender. Despite the heavy traffic back to Maryland, I was deliriously happy and much relieved.

It's often said that people's true colors emerge in the face of adversity. The fate of opening the Richmond office hinged on winning that contract. The pressure and the tenuousness of the situation would have broken the spirit of many people, but that wasn't the case with my all-star management team. My staff's enthusiasm, optimism, and cooperation were deeply ingrained and manifested in their can-do attitude. They acted as if the company was theirs; that's how determined they were to win the contract.

When LeRoy and I met with the state officials to defend our proposal, we found ourselves in the hot seat, having to justify our price, more than $300,000, which we were told was twice what they were currently paying. Acting on the tip that the procurement officer had given me about the underperformance of the current contractor, I emphasized that our price would guarantee a superior level of service that would meet their standards of cleanliness, thereby convincing them that the current contractor's lower price would only give them more of the same bad service.

Two weeks later, I received the good news that we had won the contract, which enabled us to open the Richmond office in October 1986. In the next ten years, the office grew to more than $1 million in annual revenue, until I closed it in 1996: the Richmond market proved to be very competitive, and it was too hard to maintain a profitable operation. Nonetheless, I am proud to have had the state capitol building under contract during the tenure of Governor Douglas Wilder, the first black person to be elected governor in the United States.

It took five years from the time SBA expelled me to steady my company and get it back on track, but by 1990, Centennial was on its way to a full recovery. The real boost came when we won the Dulles Airport contract through a competitive bid under the Washington Airport Authority's Local Disadvantaged Business Enterprise program. Under this program, the bidding contractor had to be a small business with annual revenues not to exceed an amount defined by the authority. The other criterion was that the contractor had to be located within a hundred miles of Washington, D.C.

At the time that Centennial was awarded the contract, the authority's revenue size standard was $10 million a year. It was later increased to $12 million. A few years later, I successfully convinced the authority to increase it to $16 million. For the next eleven years, the Dulles contract's revenues grew from $3 million to $6 million annually.

Although this was Centennial's largest contract, it did not produce the highest profit margin. By this time, my management team was used to hearing me say, "It's not the top number—revenue—that's most important; it's what flows to the bottom line—net profit." The million-square-foot Dulles facility came with a host of challenges that would give a military field general pause as he moved his troops into battle. The facility required the coordination of a staff of more than a hundred managers, supervisors, and hourly workers each day at the height of the contract.

In addition, Centennial had to make a capital investment in vehicles to transport workers around the facilities and in sophisticated equipment such as "ride-on" floor scrubbers. If it weren't for LeRoy's abilities and competence, Dulles Airport could have been a scheduling nightmare because it required workers to be on the site twenty-four hours a day, 365 days a year.

This contract was further complicated by the fact that Dulles was unionized, and our managers had to abide by the requirements of the agreement that had been negotiated with the union. To avoid paying overtime and staying within budget, my supervisors had to make sure that we had adequate hourly staff on hand at each site every day. LeRoy's performance managing a contract that represented a third of the company's $20 million in annual revenues was so extraordinary that he earned a promotion to vice president of operations.

In the meantime, remaining true to my growth strategy, I pressed on and continued to look for other expansion opportunities in the northeastern part of the country. In 1995, Centennial was hired as a subcontractor and supplier to the prime contractor for the World Trade Center in New York City. Fortunately, the contract ended a year before the 9/11 tragedy. In 1998, I also acquired a janitorial company in Boston, which opened up another market.

Despite setbacks, obstacles, and missteps, Centennial proved that it had staying power as we approached our twentieth anniversary.

In October 1996, I hosted an evening reception for more than a hundred people that included employees and their families, clients, and friends as well as my family. Although this was an impressive milestone, I was not about to rest on my laurels.

What lay ahead of me was what I considered to be the most challenging phase of my company: developing a succession plan. Without a doubt, this is probably the most delicate and complex stage of a family-owned business, especially when you have two opposing forces: nonrelatives in management positions versus family members whom you're attempting to integrate into the company. The question of who will succeed the founder is always fraught with danger. One wrong move and the situation can blow up in your face. That is exactly what happened.

A few months before I brought in a consultant to help me develop a succession plan, my youngest daughter, Tasha, joined the company. Since she had expressed an interest in the company, it was only natural for me to think that she would eventually inherit Centennial. However, I knew it wouldn't be for quite a while, because she was only twenty-three years old at the time. My older daughter, Darnetha, was not at all interested in Centennial. She is a fine-arts type whose first love is music, dance, and film. (Interestingly enough, she started a dance company at the age of thirty-six—the same age I was when I launched my company.)

In fact, right before Tasha came into the business, I had reassured LeRoy, who by then had been promoted to executive vice president, that he was in line to directly succeed me. To say that he grew in power and stature during his long tenure with the company is an understatement. Although he reported directly to me, all senior executives—vice presidents of marketing, finance, operations, and human resources—reported to him. At the height of his career as executive vice president, there was no question that he would succeed me. LeRoy had all the qualities of a leader: he knew how to motivate his staff and gain its cooperation even when he had to make tough financial decisions.

I had broached the succession plan with LeRoy, and I had made it emphatically clear that I wasn't about to hand over control of the company to my daughter, who was inexperienced and far too young—seventeen years his junior. In fact, wanting to dispel any suspicion of nepotism, I deliberately put Tasha under his charge so that he was fully responsible for training her. In fact, it was actually LeRoy who finally convinced Tasha, who was initially undecided, to join the company, because he thought it was only right that she should eventually inherit the business that her mother had worked so hard to build.

Just as I was settling into the next phase of my company and coming to terms with the concept of a succession plan, I received shocking news about the Dulles contract. I was advised that Centennial would no longer qualify to bid on Dulles when the contract expired in a couple of years because Centennial's annual revenues would have exceeded the Washington Airport Authority's revenue size requirement. My company had grown to almost $20 million in revenue, but the loss of this contract would mean a cut of $6 million in one fell swoop, almost a third of my company's revenues.

This was déjà vu all over again, bringing me back to that horrific year, 1985, when I was expelled from the 8(a) program. I was beginning to feel haunted. In 1998, I had a fleeting thought about getting out of the business but had put it out of my mind. Now, knowing that the Dulles Airport contract would expire in just three years, I began to seriously question whether I had the stomach to relive the 1985–1990 era. I thought back to the business broker who approached me a few years earlier asking me if I would consider selling the company. At the time I wasn't ready to entertain the idea, but now, with the loss of a major contract looming over me like the sword of Damocles, I was beginning to think that the time had arrived.

Compounding the prospect of the loss of the Dulles contract was another issue that I could no longer ignore. What I saw when

I stared at myself in the mirror was someone who no longer enjoyed the business. Thinking that Tasha was in good hands with my second-in-command training her to assume a managerial role in the company, I started to delegate many of the day-to-day operations to my management team. In time, some of my employees would accuse me of abdicating responsibility. In effect, my absence and lack of involvement was a sign that I had handed over control of the company to LeRoy.

I was a classic case of a leader who had become isolated and too far removed from operations, the heart and soul of a business. During the next year, my company would slip away from me like sand slipping through my fingers. Thinking that I was running out of time, I had to make some critical decisions. I could either become reengaged in the company—something I was loath to do at this stage of my life—or I could sell it.

There were other reasons for my losing interest in the company. The nature of the industry was changing, and I was facing external challenges outside my control. Many contracts were becoming unionized, which made it increasingly more expensive to do business. A union contract required higher wages than nonunion contracts did. This put me at a disadvantage in hiring hourly employees. I couldn't compete with union wages.

In addition, I was facing a new kind of competition. Start-ups were springing up that hired illegal, undocumented workers and paid them lower wages or that engaged in illegal subcontracting in which no employee benefits were paid, not even Social Security. Furthermore, the makeup of the labor pool was changing with the influx of non-English-speaking employees. To continue to compete, I would have to develop costly and extensive language-training programs to help my management staff become bilingual.

That's when I decided to take LeRoy—the person who had been with me since my first year in business—into my confidence. I set up a meeting to talk to him about the possibility of selling the company. The business relationship that we had developed over the life of the company would make a fascinating Harvard case study of how a power struggle can ultimately bring down a company. I was about to learn the most painful lesson of my career: I was ultimately responsible for having missed and ignored the warning signs of a disaffected employee.

What I thought was a successful preliminary discussion about selling the business turned out to be a disaster. I could understand that selling the company would be threatening to the person who had risen to a powerful position, but I thought I had made my intentions clear to LeRoy that he would be taken care of if I sold the company. I had emphasized that I would work with him to come up with a business arrangement that would be monetarily and professionally rewarding to him. I was even willing to consider giving him some form of cash payment or help negotiate a contract with the new owner if he wanted to stay. The only thing I had asked of LeRoy was that he keep our conversation confidential because I was just exploring this option and was not the least bit ready to execute it. I assumed that he had agreed to this request.

Instead, LeRoy returned to his office and proceeded to announce to his staff, which included my daughter Tasha, that the company was being sold. I had previously made a decision not to tell Tasha first because I wanted to float the idea by LeRoy to get his support before discussing it with her. That this young man, who started out as an hourly employee and rose to a top management position, had become my nemesis was a nightmare come true.

Facing my own demons and what I saw as the betrayal of my executive vice president left me with no recourse but to put the company up for sale. I contacted the broker who had approached me a few years earlier and asked him to find a buyer. This was after I had made a final appeal to Tasha. I promised her that I would renew my commitment to the business and train her to succeed me if she would consider staying with the company, but she would have no part of the plan. She wanted to wash her hands of the company and get on with her life.

Although I benefited financially from the sale of my company, it broke my heart to see that what had been built up over so many years had been dismantled overnight. The new owner, who appeared to be the ideal candidate, turned my family-oriented culture into a hostile environment. He retained much of my management team, including my executive vice president, but I heard that no one was getting along. As if that wasn't enough, the owner also changed the name of the company—even though the business had established a reputation and had name recognition. Neither the customers nor the vendors were familiar with the new name or the new owner. Former employees became disenchanted, and many left; others were summarily fired.

There was a silver lining to this otherwise unhappy ending. I am proud to say that Centennial prepared many of its management team members for key positions at other companies in and outside the industry. In fact, when I recently spoke with my former executive Legusta, he said that he had founded his own janitorial company, Acclaim USA, on many of the principles that were espoused at Centennial One. Cesar, my hourly employee who had once said that he wanted to become the president of Centennial One, became the director of operations of another janitorial company.

*   *   *

When Roy and I divorced in 1986, it seemed that my business life and personal life were on a collision course, and there were times when I wondered which one would do me in first. If the stress of my business was enough to break the back and the spirit of a strong woman, the stress of my personal life was enough to make a sane woman go crazy. I was a single mother living in a country house that was way too big, and I was taking care of my aging mother and two preteen daughters.

By this time, the girls were going to a private school in Annapolis, Maryland, which was far away from our home. Although they rode the bus to school, I had to drive them to the bus stop, which was about half a mile from the house. In addition, I had to shuttle them back and forth to school activities, music lessons, and various sports and social activities. There was no end to where they needed to go, and there was no relief, either. This was in addition to the demands of my business.

Then the unthinkable happened. My mother, at age eighty-five, became ill and was hospitalized to have a kidney removed. That was the beginning of her descent. She was hospitalized again a year later, and after a battery of tests, she was diagnosed with colon cancer. My siblings helped by contributing to her medical costs, but I was the primary caregiver. As her health worsened, she became my top priority. We lost our dear mother on May 19, 1987, at age eighty-seven.

If Mama had to go, she couldn't have planned a better exit. Right before her death, she had been badgering my cousin Rudy and me to plan a family reunion. Both of us had our share of excuses for not having the time to plan it, but she was so insistent that we finally agreed to do it. The first Hobson-Taylor reunion took place in August 1987. (The reunion was named after my maternal grandparents, John Hobson and Hattie Taylor.) On that day, I imagined Mama smiling down on us, saying, "Look at that big, beautiful, spirited family. And I'm up here looking over them." Our reunions still occur every two years, but Rudy and I have passed the baton to the next generation, which is now responsible for coordinating the event. As senior family members, Rudy and I sit back and enjoy our place in the sun, surrounded by two hundred of our favorite people.

*   *   *

After my divorce, my social life hit rock bottom. Why is it that as soon as you get divorced, your married friends treat you as if you have the plague? The phone calls stopped, and so did many invitations. The only membership that was open to me was the Lonely Hearts Club. There's a theory that married couples avoid socializing with newly divorced people for fear that they'll get the divorce "disease."

Through it all, however, I relied on three close friends who stood by my side: Vivian, Anna, and Trish. My friendships with these women had been formed long before I married and long before I started my company, and now they held me together when it could have been all too easy for me to fall apart. At the time of my divorce, Vivian and Trish still lived in Maryland, but Anna had moved to Florida. Nevertheless, we kept the phone lines busy.

Despite my lonely life as a single, suburban, working mother, I was determined to make the best of it. I thought back to my life before I was married and discovered that my adventurous spirit was still here—she had just been stuffed in a closet. So I took her out of the closet, dusted her off, and ventured out of the house, going solo to the theater, museums, and even parties (when I would get an invitation).

That's when I was exposed to a sport that I never thought I'd have the least interest in learning. If someone were to have said to me, "Lillian, someday you're going to be a golfer," I would have shot back, "Who are you talking to? Why would I want to waste my time chasing a stupid white ball?" Nevertheless, that's what happened. I was the chairwoman of the board of the Bowie State University Foundation when the foundation decided to sponsor a golf tournament as a fundraiser. As its chairwoman, I thought I was expected to play.

On the day of the tournament, I walked into the clubhouse and approached the registration desk with an attitude, *There's nothing to this silly little game. I'll just put my athletic ability and my competitive spirit to work. No sweat!* I was greeted in a friendly manner by a volunteer who was handling registration. "Good morning," he said cheerfully. "Are you checking in?"

"Yes, I am."

"What's your name?"

"Lillian Lincoln."

"Mrs. Lincoln, what's your handicap?"

"What's that?"

The shock on his face registered a 10 on the Richter scale. I never considered myself a comedian, but at that moment I could have upstaged Lucille Ball. He turned to one of the board members who happened to be a semipro golfer and said, "I have this lady here who wants to play in the tournament, and she doesn't even know what a handicap is."

The board member responded: "Let her play. You take her out, and I'll join you guys later."

The volunteer shook his head as he checked my name off the list. I had arrived with no clubs, golf balls, or golf shoes. I didn't even know that special shoes were required for this peculiar sport, and I assumed that clubs and balls were provided. I wasn't going to let this little oversight stop me from having a good time, however. My newfound friend took me to the pro shop so I could rent equipment and buy golf shoes. Fortunately, I was appropriately dressed in slacks and a shirt, so I didn't have to buy a golf outfit. All decked out with my new shoes and rented clubs, I felt pretty good, and I was even a bit cocky, if not confident, that I could master this sport in no time.

I was on the tee box, ready to square off, but before I could even think of swinging the club, my instructor friend stopped me and began giving me detailed instructions on the basics: how to grip the club, how to swing, how to tee up the ball, and how to position my feet. That's when it occurred to me that this game might be a bit more complicated than it looked. I thought that all you had to do was look at the ball and hit it. Was I ever wrong!

As much as I tried following his instructions, I kept missing ball after ball, swing after swing. The only things flying were divots. My instructor gave me several chances to hit the ball, but when we got to the sixth hole, he looked straight at me and said, "Lillian, you're not trying. You're not even looking at the ball. You're not checking your grip or your swing. From now on, I won't give you a second chance."

No second chance? That's all it took. From that hole through the next twelve holes, I never missed hitting the ball again. Not all my shots were good, but I learned how to swing the club and to keep my eye on the ball. As every beginner golfer knows, the sound of the club whacking the ball is as good as a hole in one when you're just learning how to play.

That evening at the awards presentation, not only did I get the prize for the worst golfer, but I also discovered that I was not part of the "official" tournament. It didn't matter, though. I had so much fun and my teacher was so patient and understanding that I signed up for golf lessons shortly after the tournament. I later learned that the golfer who had taken me out on that fateful day was an excellent golfer with a handicap of 5. This experience opened up a new world of pleasure, and to this day, I love playing golf. That I never held a golf club in my hand until the age of forty-six just goes to show that it's never too late to try something new.

Even though golf was giving me a great deal of pleasure and a newfound freedom, I was still very lonely. My loneliness was compounded by the challenges of my business during this period. Then one weekend my friend Anna introduced me to a man whom I began to date and later married. Let's just keep the story short by saying that he became my second husband for all the wrong reasons. I learned the hard way that you alone are responsible for your own happiness, and no one can give you the things you need to be satisfied. After four long years, I bailed out in 1993.

After a second failed marriage, I vowed that I would never marry again. Instead, I was determined to concentrate on my business, raise the girls, remain involved with my church, and stay close to my siblings. I lived up to that vow for four more years until my sister-in-law Shirley (Willie John's wife) decided to take matters into her own hands after I had confided in her that it would be nice to have a male friend to escort me to business functions. I had carefully selected the word *escort* because I wanted to emphasize that I was not interested in a boyfriend or, God forbid, a committed relationship.

Shirley nodded her head as if she understood exactly what I meant. She said that she had a high school friend who was recently widowed and would make a great escort. By the end of our conversation, I agreed to meet this man (or escort, in my mind), even though I believed that such a meeting would probably never take place. *Even if it does,* I told myself, *surely nothing will come of it.* True to her word, Shirley scheduled a luncheon at her house. I was set to meet John Anthony Lambert Sr. on a November afternoon in 1997.

I was a bundle of nerves the day I drove to Richmond, and I wondered why I was putting myself in the awful position of meeting this man. Apparently Willie John's reaction mirrored my own concerns. When he heard what Shirley had done, he said he wanted no part of the introduction. He asked Shirley, "What if it doesn't work?" Shirley's response was priceless: "Whether or not it works, Johnny will still be my friend, and Lillian will still be my sister-in-law." Willie John was not at all convinced, so on the weekend that I was to meet John Lambert, he conveniently decided to go to Maryland to visit his son.

My escort arrived at the scheduled time. Shirley greeted him at the door. As I walked into the living room to meet him, I gave him a careful inspection from head to toe. I quickly noticed that his sport jacket and his pants did not really complement each other, but he looked confident, with his hands in his pants pockets. I thought that he was cute; he was a bit shorter than I like, but his warm smile and pleasant voice won me over.

Shirley introduced us, and they did most of the talking throughout the meal about their school days and events in Richmond. I just listened, nodding politely when it seemed appropriate. After a couple of hours, Johnny informed us that he had to go home to rake the leaves in his yard before he left to visit his sister in Kansas City for Thanksgiving. I was offended, thinking, *I've traveled all the way from Maryland to meet him, and he has to go home to rake leaves.* I disguised my disappointment, however, resorting to typical pleasantries, saying how nice it was to have met him. Without further adieu, he left, giving no indication that he would follow up with me. Just as I had expected, it was a waste of my time.

I wanted to put this ill-fated meeting behind me and enjoy the rest of the weekend hanging out with Shirley. No sooner had Johnny left that afternoon than Shirley informed me that she had to go to the store and asked me to ride with her. On our way back home from the store, she commented, "Johnny lives just down the street. Let's stop by and say hello to him." I was not at all in favor of going to this man's house after he had expressed no interest in seeing me again. I told Shirley that in no way did I want to give him the impression that I was chasing him or that I was desperate to drum up a relationship with him. She insisted that he was not the type of person who would think less of us if we stopped by his house. I wasn't convinced, but I didn't have much of a choice because Shirley was already driving toward his house.

Sure enough, there he was in the yard raking leaves, just as he said he would be doing. He spotted Shirley's car right away and waved to us. Wearing the same big smile that he had on his face when I first met him, he invited us in for a glass of wine. It was a pleasant second meeting. On the way back to Shirley's house, I reflected on the day. He would be an interesting person to get to know, and he could be a good escort, but I didn't have the feeling that he was at all interested in getting to know me.

Meanwhile, my girlfriends in Maryland were anxiously awaiting my report of how the meeting had gone with this man. I disappointed them with my account because I had very little to share except for the observations that I had made. I decided to put him and our meeting completely out of my mind. Thanksgiving was approaching, and I made plans to visit my brothers Weldon and Clyde in New Jersey.

In the middle of the following week, my phone rang. It was John Lambert. Several telephone conversations later, followed by many social gatherings of both of our families, Johnny and I became an item. Over the next fifteen months, our affection and love for each other grew. He must have been the man I was meant to marry because all my fears and doubts about ever marrying again dissolved.

In fact, it seemed only right and natural to marry this man. He makes me laugh; he loves to cook sumptuous gourmet dinners and serve them on a table set with a linen tablecloth and napkins, good china, and lit candles—and oh, the wine! For the first time in my life, I have someone who cares about me and who loves to take care of me. He calls me his queen and treats me that way.

It took me three times to get it right, but all I can say is that at last I got it right. Johnny and I were married on April 10, 1999. When I asked my cousin Shirley if she was coming to our wedding, she responded, "I guess I had better come because it doesn't look like you are going to stop getting married until I show up at a wedding." Shirley had not attended either of my other weddings, primarily because she hates to travel, refuses to fly, and in those days did not drive. Shirley's presence put the finishing touch on our joyous wedding celebration.

Family orientation was a major consideration in my decision to marry Johnny (and it was just as important to him). He comes from a large family of four brothers (one deceased) and two sisters. They are devoted to their mother, who at the age of ninety-seven is still in reasonably good health and of sound mind. Mother Lambert, as we call her, reminds me so much of my own mother.

As the matriarch, she has welcomed me into the family and treats me like one of her own, just as she does her other daughters-in-law. Johnny's family's long-standing tradition of a family breakfast on Christmas morning—including all siblings, their children and grandchildren, which can sometimes be as many as sixty people—is an ideal replacement for my own holiday gatherings. Our immediate families are happily blended. Together we have four daughters, Joshera, Joy, Darnetha, and Tasha; one son,

John (Jay) Jr.; two sons-in-law; one daughter-in-law; eight grand-children; and one great-grandchild.

Before we were married, I informed Johnny that I like to play golf and that I'd like him to try the game. I also told him that it was okay if he didn't take to the game as long as he did not try to stop me from playing. Not only did Johnny try the game, but he also discovered that he liked it very much. Consequently, one of the perks of our marriage is that we both love to play golf together. In fact, I'd venture to say that Johnny likes the game even more than I do. Today, Johnny and I enjoy our two homes: the one we built together in Mechanicsville, Virginia, and our condo on a golf course in Sarasota, Florida.

Maryland's Lieutenant Governor Sam Bogley extends a handshake to me at
a luncheon honoring me as the recipient of the Small Business Person of
the Year for the State of Maryland award. This prestigious award is given
annually by each state. I was the first woman and the first black person to
receive this honor for Maryland, in May of 1981.

I was honored to testify
before Congress in
April of 1988 to further
the rights of female
small-business owners.

My marriage to Johnny
Lambert on April 10, 1999,
was one of the happiest days
of my life.

My surviving siblings and me at Willie John's surprise
seventieth birthday party in April of 2000 (top left to
right: Weldon, Clyde, me, and Willie John). We lost our
beloved Clyde in 2008.

Shirley Taylor Winslow (about 2000). My cousin and childhood friend, who remains the same honest, outspoken person I knew years ago.

My daughters, Darnetha and Tasha, celebrate my receiving Harvard Business School's Alumni Achievement Award in October 2003. There we are in the gardens at Dean Kim B. Clark's house.

The official photo of the recipients of the 2003 Harvard Business School's Alumni Achievement Award onstage in Burden Hall.

The celebration of my receiving Harvard Business School's Alumni Achievement Award continues with my family and friends in the gardens at Dean Kim B. Clark's house.

Johnny and me with Dean Kim B. Clark following a reception for the Alumni Achievement Award recipients.

The 35th Annual H. Naylor Fitzhugh Conference in Boston (February 2007). There I am surrounded by HBS women of the class of 2007.

11

Giving Back

The only gift is a portion of thyself.

—Ralph Waldo Emerson

On January 27, 2003, I received a letter from Harvard Business School that took me completely by surprise. The letter informed me that I was one of a few HBS graduates who were invited to receive the Alumni Achievement Award, which is the highest honor given to alumni. In his letter, then–Dean Kim B. Clark wrote the following:

> Dear Lillian: This is the highest distinction we can bestow, and you are more than deserving of it. Your enrollment at HBS and your subsequent commitment to the development of the HBS African American Alumni Association was one challenge met. Your founding and successful growth of Centennial One, Inc., a woman-owned, entrepreneurial company that has employed thousands, was yet another. The ability to break through barriers to create a new reality is a hallmark of leadership, one that your career has exemplified. Combined with your tradition of community service through local advisory contributions, you have lived the values that HBS holds at the core of its mission.

That fall, I joined the company of illustrious recipients who were feted and honored for two days with receptions, luncheons, dinners, and a panel discussion moderated by Dean Clark. The other panelists were James E. Burke (class of 1949), chairman and CEO emeritus of Johnson & Johnson; Charles O. Rossotti (class of 1964), senior adviser of the Carlyle Group and former commissioner of the Internal Revenue Service; Daniel L. Vasella (class of 1989), chairman and CEO of Novartis AG; and the leaders of the partnership of Greylock Partners, including Howard E. Cox Jr. (class of 1969), William Elfers (class of 1943), Daniel S. Gregory (class of 1957), Henry F. McCance (class of 1966), and Charles P. Waite (class of 1959).

Thirty-four years after I had graduated, I was onstage—a black female entrepreneur sitting confidently among eight powerful white male executives—waiting for Dean Clark to open the floor to the audience. I smiled to myself, recalling my days as the shy, tenuous student who struggled to raise her hand, much less her voice, in class.

A student tossed out the first question, which was not directed to a particular panelist: "Having had a successful career, who [sic] would you say had the greatest impact on your life?" I knew that question was designed for me, and I could barely contain my enthusiasm about being the first to speak. Looking out into the audience, I gazed past the heads of anonymous well-wishers and settled lovingly on my family and friends; all thirty of them who had come at their own expense to support me as I received this award. Speaking directly to them, I held my head up high and proudly announced that it was my mother and Naylor Fitzhugh who had had the greatest influence on my life.

On my graduation day in 1969, I had wanted nothing more than to get my degree, pack my bags, and put my HBS experience behind me. Now, more than three decades later, I finally acknowledged to myself that I belonged at Harvard, and I accepted the weight of my role as Harvard's first black female MBA. As I focused on the faces of my extended family, I took the award as my degree and accepted it for my ancestors, my family, and future generations of black students who would walk through the doors of Harvard Business School and leave their mark on this esteemed institution. That day I arrived at Harvard a second time, and it felt right.

*   *   *

The African proverb "If we stand tall, it is because we stand on the backs of those who came before us" comes to mind when I think of the accomplishments and contributions of many of the B-School's black alumni and affiliates, who in the past forty years have served on a variety of committees to raise scholarships and leadership awards to enhance the status of black students and black faculty. Given my relationship with Naylor Fitzhugh, I was especially honored to serve on a steering committee to establish the H. Naylor Fitzhugh professorship in honor of Professor Fitzhugh's legacy as one of the first black students to receive a Harvard MBA. Through the generous support of corporations and individuals from all ethnic backgrounds, both within Harvard and outside Harvard, we raised $5 million to establish the Fitzhugh endowment. Professor David A. Thomas is the first black tenured professor to hold the chair since it was established in 2000.

Then, of course, there's AASU, whose influential presence on campus has grown considerably since its inception, serving as an active support system for black students. Anchored in the mandate to "unite, serve, and lead," the organization remains true to the original mission of the Founding Five (which is what we five black students of the class of 1969 are called): "to furthering AASU's role within the HBS community, as well as maintaining the AASU tradition of providing activities that impact all areas of African American students' lives."

I was delighted to read on the organization's Web site that AASU takes very seriously its responsibility to address the needs of the "whole person," which is evident through the range of advice given on various topics of importance to the black experience. Thinking back on my own HBS experience, I smiled when I read that AASU offers advice on two issues: (1) providing a strategy to prepare for your first cold call and (2) offering recommendations on where to find the best barbershop or hair salon in Boston.

If only I had been given some tips on the cold call and a hair salon! Regarding the latter, my mother had shown me how to straighten my own hair (which was socially required of black women in those days) using an electric iron and curler. If she hadn't, I would surely have had to venture into unfamiliar parts of Roxbury in search of a black hair salon. No black woman would dare risk having her hair done by a hairstylist who had no experience working on black people's hair. When I was at Harvard, I remember how self-conscious I was about all the time I had to spend fussing with my hair to get it straight, whereas all my white female classmates had to do was put a comb through their hair, and it was done.

*   *   *

I have to admit that my involvement with AASU and Harvard Business School's African American Alumni Association (HBSAAA) had been sporadic, at best, in the early years after I graduated. That all changed when I saw Professor Fitzhugh at one of HBS's AASU conferences, and he made me see the errors of my way, as he always did. In his inimitable style, he questioned me about how often I came back to the school, what I was doing to help future generation of students get the most out of their Harvard experience, and what my involvement was in HBSAAA, which Fitzhugh had helped to found in 1978. Here was a man who remained true to the black cause all the days of his life. This quote from an HBS interview with Fitzhugh spoke volumes to me: "No matter what kinds of jobs you have, no matter how successful you become, you need to remember your roots as African Americans and to appreciate the extraordinary efforts of those who, from the 1940s through the 1970s, struggled to open doors of opportunity previously shut tight against all blacks."

Admitting that I had not been as active as I knew I should be, I promised him that I would support these organizations and reaffirm my commitment to be involved. HBSAAA had had some good years and some bad ones until 1997, when it was rejuvenated by the prompting of an influential black tenured professor, James Cash. In a personal letter to HBS black alumni, he urged us to take charge and energize the organization, because only a small number of black alumni had paid dues, and the organization's relationship with the school administration had become strained.

That year, Kenneth Powell (class of 1974) was elected president, and he still serves in that position. I was elected to the board and still serve as a member. Under Ken's leadership, the organization has experienced tremendous growth and influence. The association hosts many networking and educational events throughout the year, but its signature conference is the Leadership Summit, which takes place every year in the fall in a major city. Each year the summit is devoted to a particular theme on leadership.

*   *   *

Despite the progress that has been made to fortify our presence at Harvard Business School, however, I have been saddened to learn anecdotally that the size of the black student population has reached a plateau. Beginning with my class, 1969, black student enrollment had climbed steadily, but it peaked in the mid-1980s. At that point, the combined first- and second-year classes had about 150 black students, about 9 percent of the student population. After that, the numbers started to decline. In 2009, the black population was only 4 percent of the student body.

No doubt there are factors outside Harvard that have something to do with this state of affairs. Again speaking anecdotally, I think that many college-bound black students question the value of an MBA for career advancement opportunities. I suspect that the same glass ceiling that prevents women, regardless of ethnicity, from obtaining the highest office also applies to black men.

You don't have to do extensive research to see that the movers and shakers in corporate America are still predominantly white men.

The cost of an MBA is probably the number one reason that so few blacks even consider applying to the B-School. Harvard's tuition in 2009, including room and board, was approximately $80,000 a year. Without a scholarship, the average middle-class white student, much less the average middle-class black student, can hardly justify the student debt that comes with obtaining a Harvard MBA. Although the tuition of other Ivy League schools may be less than Harvard's, I'm sure that all Ivy League MBA degrees come with a stiff price tag.

Nevertheless, I can say with conviction that my Harvard MBA was certainly worth the investment and the struggle. It's true that a Harvard degree opens doors that would otherwise be closed to you. I know that my degree worked like a charm in a few tenuous business situations in which my intelligence and competence might have been called into question. I'll never know if it was because I'm a woman or because I'm black, but that was the reality that I had to face.

On those questionable occasions, all I had to do was take out my "secret weapon" and casually drop the phrase "Harvard MBA degree" into the conversation. Suddenly the atmosphere in the room would change dramatically, and people would arch their backs, sit up straight, and take notice. Although it didn't please me to resort to this kind of behavior—in fact, it upset me to think that this is what it took for people to give me a chance—I did what I had to do to preserve my integrity and self-worth as a human being.

My degree was also instrumental in helping me to get a seat at the table of public and private boards. For example, I believe that my Harvard MBA was a major consideration in Governor Mark Warner's appointing me to the Board of Visitors at Virginia Commonwealth University, which is a prestigious appointment. Of course, I would be remiss if I didn't note that being a black woman also plays in my favor for board appointments. There were times that being a double minority paid off, such as when I was appointed to the board of Citizens Bank of Maryland as a "twofer."

Hindsight is a beautiful thing, but when I'm asked what I could have done differently to make my Harvard years a more positive experience, I have to say that I wish I had reached out to my classmates and made stronger connections, not only as a student but as a career woman as well. It took me a long time and many business challenges later to understand the real power of the Harvard network. I often wonder how my company would have turned out if I had asked some of my classmates to serve as board members. I also wonder if I would have felt less isolated, particularly when I was dealing with personnel and leadership issues.

Having learned the hard way about the inherent value of developing and maintaining a network, I try to impress upon those who are eager to get ahead in both business and life to nourish their networks and keep them alive. In this age of electronic communication, especially with the rise of social media networks such as LinkedIn, Facebook, and Twitter, networking is de rigueur. I'm not speaking to younger generations, who already understand the power of networking; my pitch is to those who have not joined the electronic age of networking. To you I say try it; it's easy, it's fun, and, who knows, you may be pleasantly surprised by the connections that await you.

*　　*　　*

After I sold my company, I wasn't sure what my next step would be. I knew I didn't want to retire, so I got my real estate license and bought a tax franchise company, which was a seasonal service that helped people prepare their tax returns, primarily during tax season from January through April 15. Nevertheless, something was missing in my life. I wanted to connect with people on a more meaningful level. With more time on my hands, I began to extend my outreach into the communities that have embraced me over the years. Although I had been mentoring entrepreneurs on business matters for the past two decades, in recent years I have broadened my advice to include family, personal, and spiritual matters.

Today, my relationships as a mentor are a source of pride and joy to me when I think about how I have been able to make a difference in the lives of some very special black women. One of my oldest mentoring relationships spanned twenty years, when Sharon Dabney-Wooldridge asked me for guidance as she expanded her maid service company. It's been a pleasure to share my entrepreneurial skills and practical business knowledge and to watch her business grow into a successful full-service environmental management corporation called the Kleane Kare Team. The last time I spoke with Sharon, she was excited to tell me that she had just received her Green Cleaning Professional certification from Green Cleaning University.

Then there's Elaine Avery. I'm so proud when she introduces me as her mentor, never failing to say that my advice was pivotal in helping her achieve her goals. When I first started to mentor Elaine, she was going through some difficult times. She didn't have a job, but she had great ideas about starting a foundation to help other women. I encouraged her to hold on to her ideals and follow through on her ideas. Today, not only is she a director at First Market Bank, but she also sits on the board of a nonprofit organization, Boaz & Ruth, whose mission is to rebuild the lives and communities of people in need.

I have a special mentoring relationship with Savitri Gay, my great-niece, who was born with a fiery spirit and had entrepreneurial aspirations at a young age. My involvement with Savitri's career started when she came to work for me as an administrative assistant at Centennial One at the age of fourteen. Savitri likes to tell everyone that it was her two years' experience at Centennial that gave her insight into the world of work, which influenced her view of work from then on: "I learned very quickly that I didn't want to be an employee because I saw how Aunt Lillian worked and lived. She had freedom. She was her own boss. She was living a dream. She traveled a lot. She was the aunt who gave us money for Christmas and never forgot a birthday."

After Savitri graduated from college in 2004, she sought me out for advice about a company she had just joined. It was an entrepreneurial-oriented, full-service, financial planning outfit called Prime America. Drawing from my earlier career experience in the financial world, I played devil's advocate to help her gain a better understanding of the demands of a career in financial planning. I continue to advise her, helping her to stay focused on her ultimate goal of achieving financial independence as a successful entrepreneur. At the young age of twenty-six, she's still trying to pave a meaningful career path, but she knows that she has me as her confidant, and that gives her comfort.

Last but not least, my most recent protégé is Selena Cuffe, a graduate of HBS (class of 2003) and the founder of Heritage Link Brands, an importer and distributor of indigenous wines from Africa and its diaspora. Selena and I connected in 2007 in Boston at the thirty-fifth Annual H. Naylor Fitzhugh Conference. Much to my surprise, I was honored at a luncheon in recognition of being the first black female graduate of HBS. As a tribute, Selena's company awarded me and my husband a complimentary trip to attend the 2007 Soweto Wine Festival in Johannesburg, South Africa.

Not only was the trip the fulfillment of a lifetime dream, but it also marked the beginning of a wonderful relationship with Selena. Selena has taken the entrepreneurial plunge and has a drive and a focus that are equal to none. I can easily relate to her ambition as a businesswoman, but what really brought us together was her challenge as a working mother. She is the mother of an inquisitive infant and an energetic toddler, and I know all too well the burden she carries in trying to balance the demands of her family and her business venture.

I don't profess to have the answers, but I'm glad that I can be of help to her as a sounding board. As such, I always emphasize that there are no right or wrong decisions. Although Selena looks up to me as a role model and credits me for helping her to sort out her child-care concerns, I view our relationship as more of a sharing of two kindred spirits who are trying to lead a good life by dedicating ourselves to a higher purpose. Through our sharing of dos and don'ts about parenting, we've discovered that motherhood has not changed much, if at all, in the last few decades. In the end, I tell Selena to listen to what her heart is saying. It will let her know when she's making the right decision.

*   *   *

Although I'm no stranger to public speaking, having done a great deal of it throughout my career, at this stage of my life it feels more like a calling than an obligation. My audiences' warm reception and genuine interest in my story keep me going. It's music to my ears to hear people say that my personal journey has inspired them to dream big, act bold, and keep on striving.

One touching moment, when I felt from the bottom of my heart that my life had a higher purpose, occurred when a parishioner from my church presented me with a poem that he wrote about my being the first black woman to receive a Harvard MBA. He told me that he was inspired to write it after he had read a newspaper article about me in the *Richmond Times Dispatch*. You have to understand the backstory to appreciate how his gesture of gratitude could have had such a profound effect on me.

It started when this young man approached me one day after church had let out and said that he was so inspired by my life story that he wanted to surprise me with something special. I must have given him a quizzical look because he assured me that I would be pleased with the results. Every time I saw him in church after our initial contact, he always made a point of coming up to me to say hello with the express purpose of letting me know that he was still working on *it*. This went on for months, and finally my husband and I began to joke about the "surprise," expecting that nothing would ever come of it.

Then one Sunday, more than a year later, my fan asked me if he could come to my house to take my picture. At that point, I was more curious than anything, so I agreed. A few months later, I attended church on a Sunday when I normally would have been in our Florida home. Not expecting to see me at church, he ran up to me and said with great excitement that he had *it* in his car. I didn't understand what he was talking about, so I asked, "You've got what?" He replied, "The surprise."

Apparently, he had been carrying whatever *it* was in his car, waiting for the day that he would see me in church. I was overwhelmed with emotion when he opened the box and presented his handiwork. It was a beautifully designed plaque that included the photo of me he had taken in my home, a poem he had written about me, and icons that represented important aspects of my life: the Harvard emblem, for my MBA; a golf bag, for my love of golf; an atlas, for my world travel; African masks, for my heritage; a musical note, for my love of music; and a red rose, to symbolize universal love.

As my eyes filled with tears, he told me that he had shared his project with his young daughter because he wanted to hold me up as an example of what a person can accomplish if she is willing to reach for the stars. Today the plaque graces the wall in my office, right next to my degree from Harvard. I see my degree as the road that led me to someplace better and the plaque as the muse that inspires me to pave the way for the next generation of seekers and strivers.

Here is the poem that is on the plaque:

Lillian Lambert

> You decided to go to Harvard
> And were willing to pay the price.
> This African American woman
> Was determined to break the ice.
> Against tremendous odds
> You proudly continued to strive.
> That old African spirit
> Was there to make sure you survived.
> Centuries of our ancestors
> Were whispering softly in your ears,

"You are the chosen one.
Move ahead, we are right here."
Bound to reach great heights,
Based on your inner driving force,
Once the spirit started to guide you,
You had no choice but to stay the course.
Giving up was not an option,
And adversity you overcame.
As you paved the road for others,
You knew the pain was worth the gain.
This poem is how I honor you,
In my own very special way,
As the first African American woman
To graduate from Harvard with an MBA.

—Steve McLemore

Epilogue

Trust yourself. Create the kind of self that you will be happy to live with all your life. Make the most of yourself by fanning the tiny, inner sparks of possibility into flames of achievement.

—Golda Meir

It's mid-October 2008. I'm sitting on the lanai of my condominium in Sarasota, which overlooks a lake on the twelfth fairway of the Highlands Golf Course. I'm watching a bevy of cranes flutter along the lake's bank. On the other side of the lake is an alligator, which appears to be about four feet long. It slides and glides into the water with a graceful plop. I notice a couple who has just teed off on the twelfth hole. The man hits a long shot, but it veers off to the left into the water. The woman steps onto the tee box and hits the ball squarely, not very far, but it rolls down the right side of the fairway. I imagine their conversation based on my own good and not-so-good golf games.

He: "I can't believe I hit the ball into the water. I usually get a good tee shot on this hole. I think I'll take a mulligan." (This is a golf term that gives the player a second chance to hit a tee shot and not have the first shot count. Mulligans are permitted only in casual rounds of golf.)

She: "Okay, but I'll still give you a run for your money. Don't forget the golf cliché, It's not how you drive, it's how you arrive." (The man is probably a bit upset because his partner has had a better shot than he did. Without a mulligan, he would have been penalized because the ball ended up in the water.)

One of the reasons I enjoy playing golf is that I can draw so many parallels between the game of golf and the game of life. When I play golf and my partner allows me a mulligan, I'm grateful to him or her for giving me a second chance to start my game on the right foot. So too it is with life. Every day that I wake up in good health—a good frame of mind is a bonus—I see it as God's way of giving me a second chance to improve the life that has been given to me.

However, a second chance, in both life and golf, comes with no guarantees. We may get it right, or we may get it wrong. In both cases, it's up to us to stay focused on the goal of continuously improving ourselves and taking responsibility for the outcome. In the end, the game of life and the game of golf are a competition with oneself. In golf, it's futile to blame the weather, the ball, the terrain, or the people we play with for a bad round. In life, it does us no good to blame others when things don't turn out the way we want. Although we might not master every day or win every game, the key is to see each one as another chance to improve our game or our life.

On this particular fall day in Sarasota, my mind wanders back to the farm and my family origins. When I think of my roots, I think of my parents' hardworking hands that fed, clothed, protected, and comforted their children. We didn't have much in the way of material possessions, but we certainly had an abundance of the stuff of life that builds character: *faith* that things happen for a reason and that the course of one's life is what it is meant to be; *hope* that one has the courage to push beyond one's self-limiting beliefs and embrace a higher purpose; and *love* that inspires, heals, and binds all people together regardless of race, religion, and class.

When I think of my roots, I think of my own hands as extensions of my parents' earthbound hands touching the spirit and flesh of my daughters, Darnetha and Tasha. As my parents did for

my siblings and me, so I do for my children. I applied my parents'
practical, homespun determination to provide a better life for
their children and made sure that I gave my children a good start
in life. When Darnetha and Tasha were born, Roy and I opened an
educational fund to ensure that they would have the best education we could give them.

If a picture is worth a thousand words, an original oil painting
by John Nelson, which I acquired years ago, reflects how I feel about
learning. The painting shows a young black woman standing in a cot-
ton field with a book under her arm. She is looking toward the sky.
The caption reads "The only way out." I am that young black woman
who had to learn through trial, tribulation, and error that education
was the key to my future and a better life.

When Roy and I made the decision to send our girls to private schools, we were concerned that they would feel isolated
and estranged in a predominantly white environment, but we
were willing to take a chance because we strongly believed that
they should receive a quality education, which we thought only
a private school could offer at that time. Fortunately, Darnetha
and Tasha have an ability to adapt to their surroundings. Perhaps
it was because we've always lived in a racially mixed community,
but I like to think that it has something more to do with how they
were raised.

Love flowed freely and unconditionally in our home, with
an abundance of affirmations. Roy may have had his shortcom-
ings, but he was a loving father. His daughters were his girls, and
he would do anything to keep them safe and happy. My mother's presence and guidance over the years kept my daughters
grounded in their black heritage. They know where they came
from, and they stand proud. Then there's my love for my daughters, which is the kind of love that challenges them to stretch and
reach their full potential by being true to their own spirits and
inborn talents. Leading by example, I want them to see that they
can follow their dreams despite the obstacles they face as mothers
and career women.

Although I wanted my daughters to understand that racial discrimination exists in the American psyche, I was determined to impress upon them at an early age the notion that the best way to deal with discrimination is to hold yourself to a higher standard that debunks negative stereotypes. I espouse the Oprah Winfrey school of thought that says "excellence is the best deterrent to racism and sexism." My daughters often tell me that complete strangers compliment them on how kind, well-mannered, and thoughtful they are. They're always quick to add that it's a testament to their upbringing, which, in part, is true. But more important, it's a testament to how they evolved as human beings. In their eyes, every human being deserves to be treated with respect and dignity. It's that simple.

There was one particular incident when we lived in Davidsonville, Maryland, that shows how an act of discrimination can be counteracted with an act of kindness. One morning I looked out the window and saw a white man on his hands and knees scrubbing our driveway. I couldn't imagine what he was doing, so I asked Roy to go out and inquire. What Roy saw was our neighbor erasing a swastika. He told Roy that he had been driving by and was so offended and embarrassed by what he saw that he felt compelled to remove it, hoping that we would not see it. Apparently, we were a target of discrimination because we were the only black family in the neighborhood. I was shocked by this overt act of racism, the likes of which I had not felt since I was a child living in the segregated South. Yet, knowing that this man, a neighbor whom we didn't know well, was willing to get on his hands and knees to expunge such a vindictive gesture gave me hope and encouragement that good will always prevail over evil.

*   *   *

Throughout the many decades of my life, I have learned that if you're willing to go deep inside yourself and build a life from the inside out—rather than from the outside in—your life journey will be its own reward. The principles that resonate inside me and keep me going are these:

- There is no substitute for education, and there are no shortcuts.
- A moral compass is essential for a good life. Never compromise yourself or your values.
- Cancel your pity party. Feeling sorry for yourself accomplishes nothing.
- You can't have it all. Life is about making choices and prioritizing what is important to you.
- Live within your means. Better yet, live below your means.
- Defeat is not an option. If you're knocked down, get up and try again.
- Remain humble and never forget your roots.
- Success is a journey, not a destination. Follow your dreams and enjoy the process.

INDEX